the People's Party

SOCIALISM

THE FABIAN ESSAYS

PRIVILEGE

LABOUR   LIABOUR

CAPITAL   CAPITAL

LONDON:
WALTER SCOTT
24 WARWICK LANE

Tony Wright and Matt Carter

the People's Party

the History of the Labour Party

With 104 illustrations

Thames and Hudson

© 1997 Thames and Hudson Ltd,
London

Design by Avril Broadley

British Library
Cataloguing-in-Publication Data

A catalogue record for this book is
available from the British Library

ISBN 0-500-27956-X

Printed and bound in Spain by
Graphycems

Frontispiece: The cover of
Fabian Essays In Socialism, 1889,
edited by G.B. Shaw

On the cover, front, left to right:
1945 Election *(Popperfoto)*;
Harold Wilson and James
Callaghan, 1975 *(Hulton Getty)*;
Gordon Brown, John Prescott,
Tony Blair, Robin Cook, 1995
(Popperfoto)

Back, left to right: Poplar Borough
Council Demonstration, 1921
(Communist Party Library); Ramsay
Macdonald with J.S. Middleton
*c.*1906; Emanuel Shinwell and
Lord Hindley opening the
nationalised Murton Colliery,
Durham, 1947 *(Popperfoto)*

Contents

The Labour Party 1900– today

Introduction by
Rt Hon **Tony Blair** MP,
Leader of the Labour
Party

I very much welcome this new illustrated history of the Labour Party. It is in fact more than the tale of one party: the hundred-year history of the Labour Party tells important parts of the story of Britain in the twentieth century. From the crusade for votes for all men and women to the introduction of free education and healthcare, Labour has been there, speaking for the majority of the people and their aspirations for a better life for themselves and their children.

The strength of the Labour Party has always been its values – simple truths that hold party members together and bind them to the people of Britain. When Labour has clearly articulated these values, it has won the confidence of the British people. A fair deal; concern for those who are poor, unemployed or lacking opportunity; tolerance; and duty to others – these are great British values. They are represented in the major achievements of Labour in government. At national level Labour governments have created the welfare state crowned by the NHS, delivered high employment, extended educational opportunities to children and adults, introduced equal rights for women and ethnic minorities, and played a major role in the creation of post-war institutions that have guaranteed the peace since 1945. Meanwhile at local level, where Labour has often retained strength when it has been out of office at Westminster, Labour councils have been instrumental in creating and improving many of the services on which people depend.

The People's Party is also about the people of the Labour Party. On the wall of my office in the House of Commons is a picture of Keir Hardie, whose steadfast courage and political radicalism have provided a role model for generations of Labour people. The photographs and illustrations in this book provide a vivid record of all those outstanding men and women, from all walks of life, who have played their part in Labour's history. But behind this story of leaders and events there is also the untold story of party members and supporters up and down the country who have contributed so much not just to their party but also to the communities in which they live. They are the men and women who daily put Labour in touch with the people we wish to serve.

The story told here reminds us of two important respects in which Labour's history differs from that of the other major parties in Britain. First, we are still a young party, not yet quite a century old. Our first centenary coincides with the beginning of the new millennium. Although we have packed a lot of history into our first century, as this book reminds us, we are a product of the modern world. Second, and more significant, is the fact that unlike the other parties we were not a Westminster party that had to establish a presence in the country as democracy developed, but a party that was formed in the country and then established a presence in Westminster. We were born as a people's party; other parties had to try to become one. Labour grew out of the world of collective self-improvement and reform – the world of friendly societies, chapels, trade unions, co-operative societies, clubs and causes – and sought to give that world a political expression. That world has changed of course in all sorts of ways, but Labour's purpose in representing society's ambition for improvement remains the same.

This connects directly with a key theme of this book. The story of the Labour Party over the last generation is the story of a party that has returned to its roots, rediscovering the ideas of community, mutuality and solidarity that were the foundation of the party, and applying them in new ways to the massively changed world in which we live. Above all, it is the story of a party that has regained its identity as 'the people's party', standing up for the hopes and aspirations of the vast majority of ordinary working families, articulating the hurt and strain that is part of everyday life, and then seeking through political action to do something about it. And that applies not just here in Britain, but abroad. Internationalism is an important and valued part of our tradition.

In this project of change and renewal the party has struck a chord with the British people, who have never deserted Labour values, but sometimes doubted that the party could implement them. Now they are regaining that confidence. Just as at the foundation of the Labour Party at the turn of the century, and after 1945, and in 1964 and 1974, people increasingly believe that the Conservatives cannot take Britain forward, and they are looking to Labour to do so. Meanwhile, socialists and social democrats around the world, struggling with similar problems but in different circumstances, are looking to the British Labour Party to provide an alternative to the divisive and failed remedies of the New Right.

In the United States of America, Sweden, Italy and the Netherlands to name but four, governments of the left of centre are working to combine the power of the market with a new vision of social justice for the twenty-first century. The tide of ideas is flowing back in our direction. A new progressive era is being born.

I am proud of the way in which New Labour has taken the best of the party's values and restated them afresh for a new generation and a new world. It is because they are the people's values too that the party has seen such an influx of new members and won new support in every part of the country. We owed it to the people of this country to renew ourselves as a party, and it is clear that they understand what we have achieved. But renewing our party is only the precondition for the real task of renewing our country.

Not for the first time in its history, as this book recalls, Labour is carrying the hopes of the British people for a more decent and successful society. These hopes mean that we carry an inescapable responsibility to translate them into reality. This requires Labour to be in government, where it can develop a radical politics of the centre-left capable of meeting the challenges presented by economic and social change. It is for Labour to show that we can have both economic dynamism and social decency – and to provide an example to others. I hope this book will be read by everyone who wants to know something about Labour and its history, and about all the improvements that it has brought to Britain in the past. But it also urges us to look forward. Learning from the past will ensure that we are prepared for the future. We honour history by serving the people in government. In those moving words of my predecessor John Smith, spoken on the evening before his death: 'A chance to serve – that is all we ask'.

Chapter One
Making the People's
Party 1900–1918

When they met at London's Memorial Hall on 27 February 1900 to agree to the formation of a new Labour Representation Committee, the small gathering of socialists and trade unionists could not know how great would be the impact of their decision on British political history. At the time their goal was simply to get greater representation for working people in parliament. Their creation was not even a 'Labour Party', only a committee, without individual members and with no MPs.

Yet the formation of the Labour Representation Committee marked a significant turning-point in the political and social history of Britain. It was the birth of a political organisation which was to become the leading progressive party in Britain and the main instrument for social reform in the twentieth century.

The formation of the Labour Representation Committee (the LRC) was also the culmination of many years of political, industrial and social action. It was these historical roots that made it possible to create the LRC at the beginning of the new century and for this small parliamentary pressure group to convert itself so rapidly into a party contending for power.

In the late nineteenth century there was growing criticism of the the failings of Victorian society and their effects on the working and living conditions of the poorer classes, with mounting demands for political and social reforms. In economics, sociology, philosophy, literature, biology, even architecture, there was a ferment of new ideas and a developing consensus for radical change, even if there was as yet no clear agreement about the direction of such change.

Yet the LRC owed its birth to much more than a general climate of ideas. It required the coming together of two groups which had previously seen their interests as different, if not contradictory: the trade union movement and the socialist societies.

For the poor in Victorian Britain life was a struggle for survival. This alley in Glasgow was typical of the overcrowded and unhealthy living conditions in the working-class areas of the industrial cities, where most housing was without piped water and proper sanitation.

In the 1860s and 1870s the trade union movement had been very closely associated with the Liberal Party and opposed to the creation of an independent Labour Party. By the end of the century this had changed, and in 1899 it was the Parliamentary Committee of the Trades Union Congress (the TUC) that voted, by 546,000 to 434,000, to hold a Conference on Labour Representation, which led to the formation of the LRC.

Match girls, gas workers and 'the full round orb of the dockers' tanner'

Why the change? First there was the impact of the 'new' unionism. Before the 1880s, the unions typically represented only the skilled and better-paid workers whose jobs were more insulated from the impact of economic depression; they were in a stronger position to bargain with their employers and to pay the union subscriptions. By contrast, general labourers in sweated trades were poorly paid and easily replaced, and they were not unionised.

At the beginning of the 1880s, however, the trade union movement went through a period of rapid change with the creation of a number of 'new' unions representing mainly unskilled workers. This reached its peak with several famous strikes, such as those of the match girls and the gas workers, when previously unrepresented workers came together to form unions. In August 1889, following the gas workers' success, the dockers united to fight for better conditions and pay. John Burns led the strikers' demands for sixpence an hour, or as he put it, 'the full round orb of the dockers' tanner'.

With the growth of new unionism, the trade union movement flourished. In 1888 trade unions represented 750,000 workers. By 1892 this was one and a half million workers and by 1900 it was over two million. But, while not all new unions were as successful as the dockers, the increasing strength and militancy of the trade union movement led to a backlash by worried employers who also began to unite to protect themselves.

In 1888, the women who worked at Bryant and May's London match factory went on strike for better pay and healthier working conditions. This was one of the first successful strikes by unskilled workers.

Dockers on strike in 1889 waiting in East India Dock Road. The strike was well organised with help from other unions and the SDF, and daily marches from the East End of London to Hyde Park stirred public sympathy. After a month, the dock employers agreed to pay sixpence ('a tanner') an hour and to employ only members of the new dockers' union.

A National Free Labour Association was set up in 1893 to provide employers with non-unionised workers who would break strikes, and this was followed in 1897 by the first successful national lock-out by the Employers Federation of Engineering Associations against the Amalgamated Engineers Union. A year later in 1898 the Employers Parliamentary Council was set up to promote the interests of employers in Westminster.

With these associations and lobbying councils established, the employers also began to pursue a campaign to undermine the strength and power of trade unions through the courts. This produced a series of rulings that made unions liable for financial injuries inflicted on third parties not involved in disputes, and threatened the right of unions to picket peacefully. It became clear to the leadership of the Trades Union Congress that the only way such legal challenges could be reversed was by strengthening the representation of labour in the House of Commons.

'We have had two parties in the past: the can'ts and the won'ts, and it's time that we had a party that will'

A second reason for the change in trade union attitudes was the growing uneasiness between labour representatives and the Liberal Party. From the 1880s onwards, organised labour had representatives in parliament, elected as Liberal Party candidates but with an acknowledged right to vote with their conscience on matters of labour policy. In 1880, for example, there were three 'Lib-Labs' elected , and this group increased to eleven at the elections in 1885. However, it was for individual Liberal associations to select candidates and there was a noticeable reluctance on the part of many associations to choose men from working-class backgrounds. Keir Hardie, who had started work in the mines at the age of ten, had personal experience of such a rejection. He tried for selection as a Liberal candidate in the Mid-Lanarkshire constituency and, when he was turned down, stood as a miners' candidate. The message was clear: Labour would have to seek its own representation in parliament, independent of the other political parties.

There also appeared to be increasing political divisions between the Liberals and the unions, especially the newly formed ones. Far from representing the interests of working people, the Liberal Party was too often seen to be on the side of the employer and against the workers, as in the gas workers' strike, the Great London Dock strike and the strike at Manningham Mills in Bradford. This tendency increased when the young aristocrat Lord Rosebery became Liberal leader on Gladstone's retirement in 1894, and then in 1895 the Liberals lost power entirely, suffering a crushing defeat in the general election. There was a growing certainty in the union movement that the Liberals neither could nor would deliver the changes that working people wanted to see. As Charlie Glyde had put it, speaking at a meeting of the Manningham strikers in April 1891: 'We have had two parties in the past; the can'ts and the won'ts, and it's time that we had a party that will.'

The change in the character of the trade union movement was central to the TUC's decision in 1899 to call a conference of its parliamentary committee to examine the question of Labour representation. This conference, held the following February, was attended by some seventy organisations, most of them trade unions. On the first day George Barnes of the Amalgamated Society of Engineers, the largest union present, proposed: 'That this Conference is in favour of working-class opinion being represented in the House of Commons by men sympathetic with the aims and demands of the Labour Movements, and whose candidatures are promoted by one or other of the organised movements.' The motion was carried by 102 votes to 3, and the Labour Representation Committee was duly born, its task to advance legislation in parliament 'in the direct interests of labour'.

Yet it would be a mistake simply to say, as Ernest Bevin once famously did, that 'the Labour Party was born out of the bowels of the TUC'. The leading role was played by the unions, but those who called themselves socialists also contributed to the making of the new party.

Social Democrats, Fabians and the Independent Labour Party

Socialism in the 1880s was still a new concept. As yet Karl Marx was not widely heard of, at least in Britain. Better known were the writings on co-operative communities of Robert Owen and the radical journalism of Robert Blatchford, the Christian socialism of F.D. Maurice and Charles Kingsley, and the artistic socialism of John Ruskin. There were also three

The great designer and craftsman William Morris (standing fifth from the right) was a utopian socialist whose views were deeply influenced by his hatred of mass-production and capitalism. He joined the SDF in 1883, but left after disagreements with its leader Hyndman to form the Socialist League from the Hammersmith branch of the SDF.

newly formed socialist organisations that played a direct role in the setting-up of the LRC and so of the Labour Party.

There was the Social Democratic Federation (SDF), which had been formed in 1881 as the Democratic Federation and saw itself as the carrier of Marxism to Britain. Even at its peak, the SDF remained a small organisation, a mixture of working-class radicals and middle-class intellectuals who shared a belief in wholesale nationalisation and class politics. At its head was the top-hatted and frock-coated figure of Henry Hyndman, one of the few socialists in Britain at this time who had read Karl Marx and wrote extensively on Marxism. Indeed, Hyndman and his work earned the wrath of Marx himself, who accused Hyndman of pilfering *Das Kapital* and passing off its ideas as his own.

Marx's daughter Eleanor and the great designer William Morris were SDF members for a time, and the organisation succeeded in establishing branches in towns and cities in many parts of Britain. But for all these efforts, it never achieved a real political breakthrough. In the election of 1885, for example, the SDF's two candidates, standing in the divisions of Hampstead and Kennington wards, only managed to secure a total of 59 votes between them. The SDF was present at the February 1900 conference, putting forward a resolution that the new Committee should be 'based upon a recognition of the class war, and having for its ultimate object the socialisation of the means of production, distribution and exchange'. But this was defeated and within a year the SDF had withdrawn its affiliation to the LRC .

A more enduring influence came from the Fabian Society. Founded in 1884, the Fabians were also a small group of London-based intellectuals, led by the as yet unknown dramatist, George Bernard Shaw. Shaw brought into the group Sidney Webb and Sydney Olivier and, along with Annie Besant (who later helped to organise the match-girls' strike), they began to write pamphlets and hold meetings on the nature of socialism. Their first real public recognition came with the publication of *Fabian Essays in Socialism* in 1889, which set out the distinctive Fabian brand of evolutionary socialist collectivism.

The Fabian Society's political outlook was a combination of ethical socialism and rational collectivism, but it was distinguished from the SDF by its gradualist approach and rejection of class politics. For a long time, under the influence of Sidney and Beatrice Webb, the society also advocated a strategy of permeation through other parties rather than

'The Irresistible Momentum' of Socialist Ideas

The historic ancestry of the English social organisation during the present century stands witness to the irresistible momentum of the ideas which Socialism denotes. The record of the century in English social history begins with the trial and hopeless failure of an almost complete industrial individualism, in which, however, unrestrained private ownership of land and capital was accompanied by subjection to a political oligarchy. So little element of permanence was there in this individualistic order that, with the progress of political emancipation, private ownership of the means of production has been, in one direction or another, successively regulated, limited and superseded, until it may now fairly be claimed that the Socialist philosophy of today is but the conscious and explicit assertion of principles of social organisation which have been already in great part unconsciously adopted. The economic history of the century is an almost continuous record of the progress of Socialism.

Sidney Webb, 'Historic', from *Fabian Essays in Socialism,* ed. G.B. Shaw, 1889

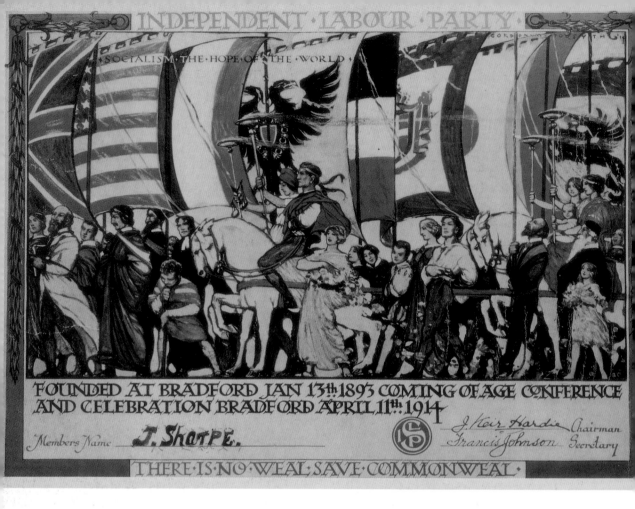

INDEPENDENT · LABOUR · PARTY

· SOCIALISM · THE · HOPE · OF · THE · WORLD ·

FOUNDED AT BRADFORD JAN 13th 1893 COMING OF AGE CONFERENCE
AND CELEBRATION BRADFORD APRIL 11th 1914

Members Name   J. Sharpe.

J. Keir Hardie Chairman
Francis Johnson Secretary

· THERE · IS · NO · WEAL · SAVE · COMMONWEAL ·

In 1914 the Independent Labour Party celebrated its twenty-first anniversary. The souvenir membership card, with its message, 'Socialism the Hope of the World', is designed in the period's heroic style. It is signed by its founder and chairman Keir Hardie.

the establishment of a separate socialist party. It was only when this approach appeared fruitless that the Fabian Society began to support the idea of a new organisation, and it was therefore also represented (by the society's secretary Edward Pease) at the Labour Conference in 1900.

Last but not least, there was the Independent Labour Party (ILP). Formed in 1893, largely as a result of the Manningham Mills strike, the ILP had a socialist programme but also sought to gain greater representation for workers in the House of Commons. It was by far the biggest of the three socialist groups, with a membership of around ten thousand from 1895 to the turn of the century. But although the ILP put forward large numbers of candidates in parliamentary elections, there was little immediate electoral success. For example, the ILP stood 28 candidates in 1895, though none of them was successful.

The ILP played a key role in the 1900 Labour Representation Conference and its contribution was crucial in two particular respects.

Firstly, it acted as a bridge between the socialists and the conservativism of some of the older unions. Some socialists, including the SDF, wanted a Labour Party represented only by the working class and committed to class war. Some of the older trade unionists did not want an independent party at all. The ILP offered a compromise, namely that parliamentary membership would be open not only to the working class but also to those who shared its interests. The committee would have whips and a policy but they could co-operate with other political parties if that furthered the interests of labour. This compromise succeeded in bringing together the interests of the trade unions and the socialist groups in a way which satisfied both.

Secondly, there were certain individuals in the ILP delegation to the conference who played a major part of the formation of the LRC; most notably James Keir Hardie and James Ramsay MacDonald. Both had experienced a desperately poor Scottish upbringing, both were strong Liberal sympathisers who had become critical of the role of the Liberal Party, and each has since been nominated as the key figure in the formation of the Labour Party. In fact Keir Hardie and Ramsay MacDonald played different but equally important roles.

Keir Hardie's reputation as the prophet leading Labour to the promised land is probably exaggerated, but this proudly independent, self-educated Scot, who had worked in the coalpit from childhood and then in journalism, certainly played a vital role in the formation of the LRC. He was involved in the new unionism movement, and had helped to establish miners' unions in Ayrshire and in his birthplace of Lanarkshire. As a young man, Hardie's politics were distinctly Liberal, albeit with a radical tinge. But he became less sympathetic towards the Liberal cause as every year passed. In 1886 he resigned as editor of the Liberal *Cumnock News* and began working full-time for the Miners' Union, where he set up his own weekly paper, the *Labour Leader.*

The real turning-point came in 1888, when the Liberal Party rejected Hardie as a candidate in the Mid-Lanark by-election; within a few months he had

The text of this pamphlet by Keir Hardie first appeared in his *Labour Leader*. It was written to help the 'average politician to calculate whether or not' the ILP (founded by Hardie in 1893) 'was likely to prove permanent or is merely the outcome of some temporary aberration which will pass away as the years bring wisdom' to the 'young men in a hurry'.

4th Edition.

YOUNG MEN IN A HURRY.

WHY THEY ARE IN A HURRY, AND WHAT THEY ARE IN A HURRY ABOUT.

BY KEIR HARDIE.

"The I.L.P. is chiefly composed of . . . young men in a hurry."—*Popular Delusion.*

PRICE, - - - - ONE PENNY.

PRINTED AND PUBLISHED BY THE
LABOUR LEADER, 53 FLEET STREET, LONDON, E.C., and 4 WEST NILE STREET, GLASGOW.

Promoting a Good Life

If men live together, forming tribes, nations, communities, societies, like stones accumulated in heaps, Society is only a collection of separate men, laws are only rules preventing their hard corners from knocking against the sides of their neighbours, the State exists only to maintain the heap (and not that necessarily). In such a unity the individual man alone counts. Individualism must be the predominating idea. Liberty is the freedom of action of the individual, and is a thing of quantity, every limit imposed on its extent – as for instance the legal command, 'Thou shalt not kill' – being a curtailment of it.

If, however, Society is a unity of the organic kind, totally different conclusions follow. The individuals composing it are still separate and conscious, but they depend very largely upon the Society in which they live for their thoughts, their tastes, their liberties, their opportunities of action, their character – in brief, for everything summed up in the word civilisation. It is in Society, and not in the individual, that the accumulation of the race experience is found. Liberty is a matter of quality and not of quantity, and curtailment of its limits does not necessarily lessen its amplitude. The community enters at every point into the life of the individual, and the State function is not merely to secure life, but to promote good life.

J. R. MacDonald, *Socialism and Society*, 1905

set up the Scottish Parliamentary Labour Party. He was not successful as a Labour candidate in Mid-Lanark, but four years later, in 1892, was elected as an Independent Labour MP for West Ham in London. This position enabled him not only to launch a powerful crusade against the poverty and social conditions of the great mass of the population, but it also provided him with a platform to argue the case for independent Labour representation. Hardie was the main force behind the creation of the Independent Labour Party and a major figure in the conversion of the TUC to the idea of separate representation in parliament.

Ramsay MacDonald's role was also central. Unlike Hardie, his education had enabled him to move away from his home town to work in England, first in Bristol and then in London, and it was during this period that he became a convert to socialism. However, he still believed that the Liberal Party provided the best route for political reforms, and for a time worked for the Liberal MP Thomas Lough. It was only when he was rejected as a Liberal candidate for Southampton that MacDonald joined the newly formed Independent Labour Party and stood as a Labour candidate. In a letter published in the *Southampton Times*, 11 August 1894, quoted in David Marquand's biography of MacDonald (1977), he identified the significance of what was happening:

The fact that your town has two members gave the Liberals an oppor- tunity of running a purely Labour candidate. They might have done this without much damage to themselves locally and they would certainly have won the gratitude of the parliamentary leaders of their party. They decided otherwise. Two commercial men are to champion what was once a progressive cause....

Just at the time when your Liberal Council plunged you into your difficulties you were hearing of similar things in scores of other con- stituencies throughout the country. Mid-Lanark Liberals refused a Labour candidate; the Liberal Association of Newcastle upon Tyne was scouring the face of the earth for a capitalist to oppose the nominee of the Trades Council; at Wigan Mr Aspinall who contested the constituency at the last election was being opposed by a Liberal candi- date; at Huddersfield, Bradford, Manchester, Bolton, South Shields, Glasgow and elsewhere the same state of things existed; and to crown all came Attercliffe. In deference to such overwhelming evidence you had to make up your minds that local Liberal Associations had cast themselves adrift from the forward movement in politics, and that the decision of the Southampton Liberal Council was but part of a national policy which is compelling what was once the advanced wing of Liberalism to sever itself from an old alliance and form itself into a independent Labour party.

MacDonald was active in many political organisations in the 1890s. He was elected to the Fabian executive in the spring of 1894, became the Honorary Secretary of the Rainbow Circle, a society for progressive thinkers, in 1896 and of the National Administrative Council of the ILP. But he was also gaining a reputation as Labour's political theorist, publishing numerous articles and books explaining his view of evolutionary socialism and of the relationship between the individual and society under socialism.

So it was the two Scots, Hardie and MacDonald, who were the architects of the movement for independent Labour representation. In 1899, with Keir Hardie, MacDonald formulated a policy for the Independent Labour Party which was critical of the Liberal Party but at the same time called for Liberals not to stand in ILP seats. And whether or not it is true that together they wrote the decisive resolution which the Amalgamated Society of Railway Servants put to the TUC in 1899, both were certainly very active behind the scenes, making sure that their hope for an independent party of labour came to fruition.

If the formation of a Labour Representation Committee was a remarkable event, even more remarkable was the way in which the LRC managed to transform itself in a matter of years from a small parliamentary pressure group into a Labour party contesting the Liberal Party as the main challenger to the Conservatives.

Having succeeded in getting agreement to form a new committee, Hardie and MacDonald were then faced with the reality of the organisation they had created. Individuals could not join the LRC, and membership was only through organisations affiliating to the committee. In the period immediately after February 1900 few unions affiliated, partly because of some continuing scepticism about the nature of the enterprise and also because the unions' decision-making process was a lengthy business. By May 1900 the LRC had chalked up only 187,000 affiliated members.

Worse still was the financial position of the Committee. The nature of the compromise arrived at by the first conference in order to win over doubting unions meant that trade unions only had to pay ten shillings for every thousand members. This meant that the LRC could not afford any staff, and that its secretary MacDonald worked without pay. Furthermore, the executive of the organisation that would shortly be contending for government held its initial meetings in MacDonald's small flat in Lincoln's Inn Fields that was so cramped that one member had to sit on the coal scuttle.

Financial constraints also meant that the LRC could not afford to put forward its own candidates. At its first big electoral test, the general election of 1900, its 15 candidates stood on the programme of their own affiliated organisations, which paid their expenses. The Labour Representation Committee's total expenses for the election came to the princely sum of £33! The results were no less modest. Despite the success of eight Lib-Lab candidates, only Keir Hardie was elected under true LRC colours. For six years Hardie, MP for Merthyr Tydfil, was the sole symbol of labour representation in the House of Commons, thereby referred to by some wags as the United Labour Party.

The first real turning-point for the new organisation was the celebrated Taff Vale judgment. In 1901 a court decision ordered the Amalgamated Society of Railway Servants to pay £23,000 for damage caused to the Taff Vale rail company during a strike. The clear implication of the decision was that unions would have to foot the bill for any strikes engaged in by their members. This struck at the heart of the whole trade union movement.

Just as legal decisions in the 1890s motivated unions towards independent representation in parliament, so the Taff Vale judgment led to a rush of union affiliations to the LRC. Affiliated membership, which stood at 350,000 in 1901, rose to 450,000 in 1902 and 850,000 in 1903. A mass movement was being forged.

This helped to strengthen the leadership's hand in negotiations with the affiliated

The Taff Vale judgment of 1901 ordering a rail union to pay for strike damage, was the culmination of several decisions in the courts that threatened workers' collective action against employers. As a result, more unions affiliated to the LRC swelling its financial resources.

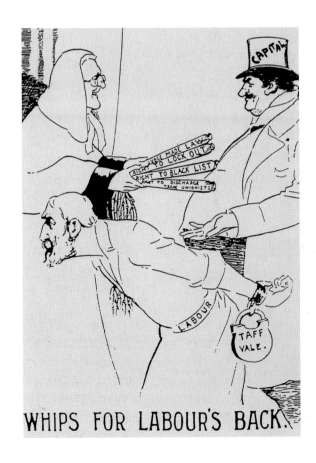

WHIPS FOR LABOUR'S BACK.

Labour's 1903 pact with the Liberals is the subject of this Will Dyson cartoon. Ramsay MacDonald leads the party on the way to Nowhere, into the Land of Compromise, saying, 'Forward, my four-footed brother, forward… and let us take advantage, in the devilish diplomatic way we are at present doing, of the fact that this Old Party is going in the same direction!'

organisations. At the LRC conference in 1903, the cost of affiliation rose to almost five pounds for each thousand members, and unions were forced to set up a compulsory parliamentary fund to pay MPs. This increase in revenue enabled the LRC to afford to pay for its own candidates, and therefore to put up people of its own choice rather than just those of the bigger trades unions. In giving financial support, the LRC was also able to make more political demands of its candidates. According to the committee's new rules, members were to 'strictly abstain from identifying themselves with or promoting the interests of any section of the Liberal or Conservative parties'.

Yet even though its membership was growing, MacDonald recognised that the electoral prospects for the LRC were bleak, and, he began secret negotiations with Liberal Chief Whip Herbert Gladstone to form an electoral pact. In 1903 the two men agreed on 50 seats where the Liberal Party would not field candidates at the next election, in return for MacDonald's agreement not to put up Labour candidates elsewhere.

1906: The LRC wins 29 seats and becomes the Labour Party

This was clearly a good deal negotiated for the committee, and in the 1906 elections, which produced a handsome Liberal victory, 29 of its 50 candidates were elected, including MacDonald himself and Philip Snowden who was chair of the ILP from 1903 to 1906. The election was a turning-point for the future of the people's party. The new grouping in parliament could for the first time elect a chair, Keir Hardie, as well as officers and whips. And the new MPs agreed on another important change — the Labour Representation Committee was henceforth to be known by a new name: the Labour Party.

With its 29 MPs, the new Labour Party was able to exert some influence in the 1906–14 parliaments, especially in the drafting of the 1906 Trades Disputes Act, which reversed the Taff Vale decision. It also gained from a late affiliation. The Miners Federation of Great Britain threw in its lot with Labour in 1908, adding a substantial number of affiliated members and 12 additional MPs.

The impression of growing electoral strength could not, however, disguise the political cost of MacDonald's pact with the Liberals. The

This photograph of the Labour Party in the House of Commons, was taken in 1911, the year that, through an agreement between Lloyd George and MacDonald, the Commons first voted for a state salary for MPs. The veteran Labour pioneer Keir Hardie, white-haired and white-bearded, is third from the right in the second row.

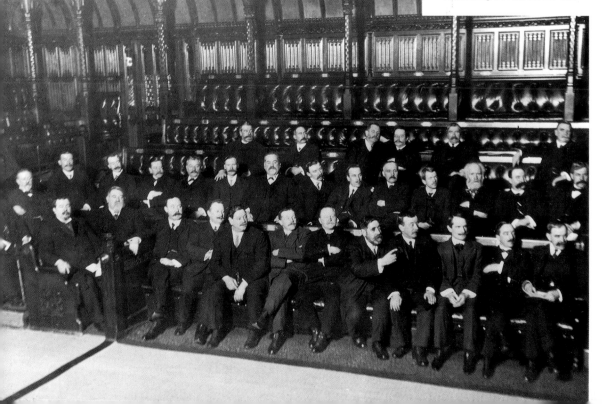

Labour Party certainly gained from the agreement, but it also became dependent on the Liberal Party's goodwill for its continued existence. And while Labour made some ground electorally, there was no evidence that it would be able to beat Liberal candidates in a three-way contest.

Worse still, the Osborne decision of 1909, so called because of the complaint of one railway union member about the use of his union subscriptions, prevented union money being used to fund the Labour Party. Thrown into financial crisis by this decision, the party hoped that the Liberals would not call a general election.

Unfortunately for MacDonald, Hardie and the rest of the party, the Liberals called not one but two elections in 1910 in order to resolve the constitutional crisis with the House of Lords which had used its power of veto to block Liberal legislation for tax reforms. The pact held for sitting Labour MPs, but almost all other Labour candidates had to stand against both Tory and Liberal opposition. Labour won in only a handful of seats where the pact did not apply, and the Liberals actually took 6 seats from Labour. Moreover the number of candidates the party could afford to stand dropped from 78 in January 1910 to 56 in December. Clearly the financial crisis was taking its toll.

To try to solve this, MacDonald made an agreement with Lloyd George: a promise of support for his Insurance Bill in return for legislation to provide for the state payment of MPs. In 1911 the Commons voted members an annual salary of £400. Further improvement came with the passing of the 1913 Trade Union Act, which enabled unions to use money for political purposes, provided they kept the funds separate. These extra resources enabled the Labour Party to expand its organisation. The number of constituencies affiliated rose from 73 in 1906 to 179 by 1914. The party was also able to expand its full-time staff, and for the election expected in 1914 Labour looked set to put up a record 150 candidates.

Yet politically the party was still weak in 1914. The previous eight years of Liberal government had been dominated by constitutional matters and the question of Home Rule for Ireland, on which the new Labour members had little to say, or the passing of a number of positive social reforms (the introduction of old-age pensions and insurance for health and unemployment, for instance), of which the Labour Party could offer little criticism. In any event, Labour was still dependent on the electoral support of the Liberals for its successes, and between 1910 and 1914 it lost a number of by-elections, significantly reducing its parliamentary representation. By the outbreak of war in 1914, there was certainly no guarantee that the Labour Party would break the existing two-party stronghold.

It was the First World War that changed the face of British politics. The outbreak of the conflict in 1914 had a direct impact on the Labour Party itself. Its former leader and passionate international socialist, Keir Hardie, died a broken man in 1915. MacDonald, also a pacifist and internationalist, resigned as Chairman of the Parliamentary Party and, with a number of ILP colleagues and Liberal members, he founded the Union of Democratic Control, which issued anti-war propaganda. His deep convictions and courageous stance against the war were to cost MacDonald his Leicester constituency in 1918, and a by-election in Woolwich. It was not until 1922 that the British public forgave MacDonald, when he was elected as MP for Aberavon.

The Old Age Pension Act of January 1909, a Liberal reform, is portrayed here as the 'New Year's boon to the aged Poor'. Before the state pension, the old were often refused Poor Law out-relief, and ended their days in the workhouse. All British subjects over seventy with an income of less than £31.10s a year had the right to a pension.

MacDonald was replaced as Parliamentary Party chair by Arthur Henderson. An ironfounder and trade unionist in Newcastle, Henderson was first elected to parliament in the 1903 by-election in Barnard Castle, where he defeated a Liberal and a Tory. Politically, he represented the school of new unionists who shifted allegiance from the Liberals to Labour in the 1890s. He became the party's secretary in 1911, and it was Henderson who worked to ensure that Labour's organisation not only survived but grew and strengthened, despite the Osborne judgement and by-election defeats.

In addition to the changes in the leadership of the party, there was also an increased political profile. The great demands that war placed on industry and the economy meant that the Liberal government was particularly anxious to keep the support of the unions, and in 1915, Henderson was invited to join Asquith's coalition government as President of the Board of Education. This also included a seat in cabinet and, with two other Labour MPs taking junior offices in the Treasury,

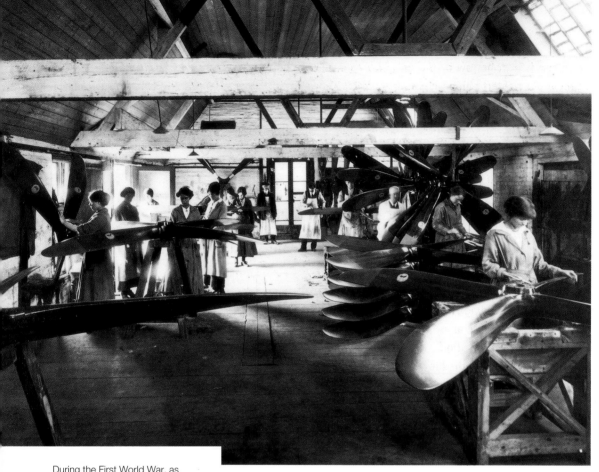

During the First World War, as more men were conscripted into the fighting forces, and war made heavy demands on industry, more women were needed on the shop-floor. In this Ipswich company producing aeroplane propellors the workers were mostly women.

the standing of the Labour Party was substantially increased.

But the most dramatic impact of the war was on the Liberal Party, an impact described by one commentator as equivalent to being hit by a runaway bus. Asquith managed to cling on to power for the first two years of the war, but his coalition government collapsed in December 1916, and Lloyd George was invited to form an administration with Conservative support. The Parliamentary Liberal Party split, half following Asquith, the other half throwing in their lot with Lloyd George. This precipitated a post-war exodus to Labour of many radical Liberal party members who repudiated a party that had become so closely associated with such Tories as Bonar Law and Lord Curzon.

Henderson joined the five-man war cabinet, an action backed by the party at its 1916 conference. But a year later, in 1917, Henderson's concern at the growing turmoil in Russia after the February revolution and his desire to attend an international socialist conference in

Stockholm (which he saw as the only way to ensure a constitutional regime in Russia) left him on the doorstep of 10 Downing Street while the cabinet met in secret. Although Henderson resigned, it was effectively a dismissal by Lloyd George and his Conservative colleagues. Yet Henderson was to have the last laugh, for by his action Lloyd George had set in train the events that were eventually to sink the Liberal Party and open the way to Labour.

Constitution and Clause IV; Labour and the new social order

Out of the cabinet, Henderson devoted his energies to making the Labour Party ready to fight an election once the war was over. He had long been dissatisfied with the way the party was structured, and so, with the help of leading Fabian, Sidney Webb, drew up a constitution for the Labour Party and an accompanying political programme.

Labour's new constitution, adopted at its London conference in February 1918, included the famous 'Clause IV'. This declared the party's commitment to 'common ownership of the means of production and the best obtainable system of popular administration and control of each industry or service' (the commitment to common ownership of the means of 'distribution and exchange' was added in 1928). Less well known, although it was seen as far more important at the time, is that the 1918 constitution allowed individual men and women to join the Labour Party for the first time. This not only changed Labour's internal structures, but it also represented a significant shift in the party's purpose, symbolising the fact that Labour was no longer simply a pressure group for the trade unions, but a national party seeking to appeal to those who worked 'by hand and by brain'. Labour was on its way to becoming the people's party.

The attempt to broaden Labour's appeal was backed up by *Labour and the New Social Order,* the political programme written by husband and wife, Sidney and Beatrice Webb, whose advocacy of efficient economic and social planning had dominated Fabian theory and influenced the London School of Economics (the LSE) which they had helped to set up in 1895. The programme put forward four policy goals: a National Minimum, including full employment and a minimum wage; the democratic control of industry, including the nationalisation of mining and the railways; the proper funding of social services, through progressive

Labour's Political Programme: the Four Pillars

The Four Pillars of the House that we propose to erect, resting upon the common foundations of the Democratic control of society in all its activities, may be termed, respectively:

a **The Universal Enforcement of the National Minimum;**
b **The Democratic Control of Industry;**
c **The Revolution in National Finance; and**
d **The Surplus Wealth for the Common Good**

What the Labour Party stands for in all fields of life is, essentially, Democratic Co-operation; and Co-operation involves a common purpose which can be agreed to; a common plan which can be explained and discussed, and such a measure of success in the adaptation of means to ends as will ensure a common satisfaction. An autocratic Sultan may govern without science if his whim is law. A Plutocratic Party may choose to ignore science, if it is heedless whether its pretended solutions of social problems that may win political triumphs ultimately succeed or fail. But no Labour Party can hope to maintain its position unless its proposals are, in fact, the outcome of the best Political Science of its time; or to fulfil its purpose unless that science is continually wresting new fields from human ignorance. Hence, although the Purpose of the Labour Party must, by the law of its being, remain for all time unchanged, its Policy and its Programme will, we hope, undergo a perpetual development, as knowledge grows, and as new phases of the social problem present themselves, in a continually finer adjustment of our measures to our ends. If Law is the Mother of Freedom, Science, to the Labour Party, must be the parent of Law.

Labour and the New Social Order, 1918

YESTERDAY - THE TRENCHES

TO-DAY - UNEMPLOYED

taxation; and the reinvestment of any surplus into education for the common good of all. The programme was hugely influential, and remained the cornerstone of Labour's policy for a generation.

So by 1918, in its eighteenth year, the Labour Party came of age. It had a new constitution and a distinctive programme, both enabling it to appeal to the nation and not just to a section of society. Its leading members had gained experience of government during the war, without associating themselves too closely with the conduct of the conflict. The party was also growing in electoral strength. In the post-war election of 1918, Labour fielded a record 388 candidates, winning 63 seats. While this total may have been disappointing, it was significant that in another 79 seats Labour came second, ahead of the Liberals. Labour was on the verge of replacing the Liberals as the second major party in Britain. As Walter Hines Page, the US ambassador, wrote to President Wilson in 1918: 'The Labour Party is already playing for supremacy'.

Two Labour posters that recall the harsh reality for many working-class men after the war. Many of those who had survived the trenches soon faced unemployment, and war veterans and their families were often reduced to begging in the streets.

Chapter Two
From Protest to Power
1918–1931

In 1918 the new Labour Party had come of age. It had stepped out from the shadow of the Liberal Party and now faced the newly enlarged electorate on its own account. But its electoral performance in 1918, winning only 63 seats and losing many of its leading figures, including MacDonald, Snowden, and Henderson, showed that it still had a mountain to climb. J.H. Thomas of the railway union and J.R. Clynes, founder member of the ILP and leading member of the National Union of General and Municipal Workers, were the only men of note left in parliament. Willie Adamson, the undistinguished Scottish miner, was elected chair of the Parliamentary Labour Party (the PLP).

Within parliament the first few years after the war represented a step backwards, a period of drift and little progress. But outside parliament, the party was continuing to grow in organisational strength, with the number of local parties rising from 239 in 1916 to 492 by early 1920. Labour's strength was developed in former Liberal areas such as Lancashire and consolidated in other urban areas. The party also made a pitch to capture the votes of the women who were newly enfranchised after the 1918 Representation of the People Act. The Women's Labour League had been set up in 1906 to recruit women to the party, with a membership of 5500 in 1918 and growing to 200,000 by 1925.

Lloyd George had won the 1918 general election, at the head of a coalition of Conservatives and Liberals. His policies, however, including the treaty of 1921 creating the Irish Free State in southern Ireland, antagonised the Conservatives within the coalition. By 1922 they had decided that they no longer needed Lloyd George's leadership and they dumped him, forcing an election in which his National Liberal group was culled from 133 to 62. The Conservatives won a handsome victory, taking 345 of the seats in parliament, but it was Labour's result that was the most impressive; at a stroke it had doubled its parliamentary

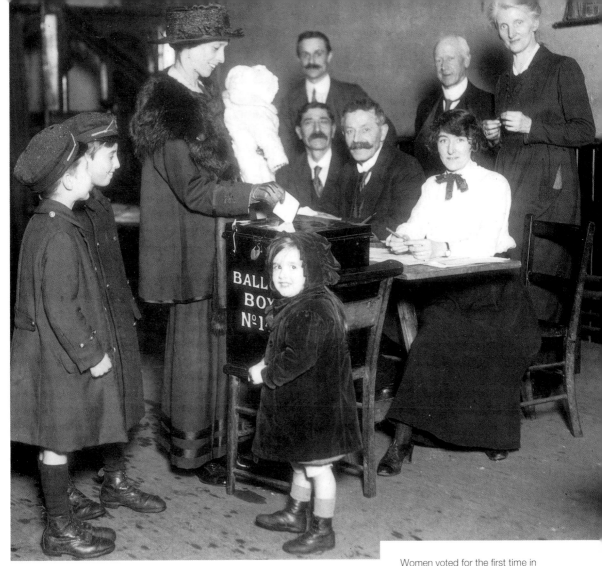

Women voted for the first time in the election of December 1918. The sensational tactics of the suffragettes stopped when war broke out, and it was women's contribution to the war effort that led to the Act of 1918 which gave the vote to all women over thirty who were ratepayers or married to ratepayers.

representation, winning 142 seats and increasing its vote from 2.4 million to 4.2 million. For the first time in its short history, Labour was the second largest party and duly occupied the opposition benches.

There was a double significance about the 1922 intake. Firstly, the new MPs were from a more varied background, both politically and socially. Of the 142, only 85 were sponsored by trades unions, 32 by the ILP, 4 were former Liberal MPs, 21 were university graduates and 9 had been to public school. Secondly, 1922 saw a return to parliament for Ramsay MacDonald and Philip Snowden, absent since 1918, while new entrants included Sidney Webb and Major Clement Attlee, an Oxford graduate turned to socialism by voluntary work in the Stepney slums,

THE WEBB OF DESTINY.

Sidney Webb entered parliament as a new Labour MP in 1922. In this *Punch* cartoon of 1923 he carries the red hazard flag before the steamroller of Fabian socialism with the words: 'I am waving this red flag, not provocatively, but to signalise what I have so happily called the inevitability of gradualness which marks our roller's advance.'

who had lectured at LSE before serving in the war. Henderson was again defeated, but returned in a by-election in January 1923.

MacDonald was elected chair of the party, a position from which he put all his energies into making sure that Labour grasped its opportunity as the main opposition party. This was not always easy with a Parliamentary Party in many ways more suited to backbench criticism and pressure-group politics than the more demanding role of His Majesty's Opposition. On a number of occasions MacDonald had to admonish colleagues about their behaviour in the House of Commons, as in April 1923 during a debate when a handful of Labour members sang the socialist anthem 'The Red Flag' in the chamber in protest at the government's actions. Another group, including James Maxton and John Wheatley, was censured for using unparliamentary language that would make today's exchanges across the chamber seem positively restrained by comparison. But MacDonald largely succeeded in his attempt to make Labour look like the government-in-waiting; and the snap election in December 1923 gave Labour its first chance to exchange protest for power.

The first Labour government: the party in power

The Conservative administration had been dogged by rising post-war unemployment. Having been previously committed not to implement tariff reforms, their new leader Baldwin felt that British products must be protected against cheaper imports to reduce unemployment. The Liberal Party had now reunited and was strongly opposed to protective tariffs. MacDonald feared that by making the election a plebiscite on the issue of protectionism, the Liberals might regain some ground and threaten Labour's gradual advance. Labour and the Liberals were now fighting for the right to be the official second party in British politics, a status that brought with it huge electoral advantages.

Labour fears were dissipated with the result of the election. The party won 191 seats, 49 more than in 1922. The Liberals also did well, winning

159 seats, at the expense of Baldwin's Conservative Party, now reduced to 258 MPs. As the election had been fought on a single issue, and Baldwin had failed to obtain the mandate he sought, it was Ramsay MacDonald who was asked by the king to form a government. It was a momentous time, both for the party and the country.

But it was not immediately clear whether Labour would take the opportunity it had been given. Some within the party counselled MacDonald against forming a minority government, which would be dependent on the Liberals for its support and unable to carry out a socialist programme. The Liberals seemed to hold the same view. After the 1923 election result, Asquith smugly informed Liberal colleagues, 'Whoever may be for the time being the incumbents of office, it is we…who really control the situation.'

MacDonald knew the significance of Labour's predicament. If the party refused office, he was sure that the Liberals would not. A Liberal government would mean that the Conservatives would become the

In the early 1920s, the Labour council of Poplar, one of the poorest London boroughs, took action to highlight the inadequacy of the Poor Law now that long-term unemployment was rising. In Poplar eligibility for out-relief (cash payments funded by local rates) was generously interpreted. Thirty Poplar councillors went to prison in 1921 for refusing to pay the central levy due to LCC, thus achieving some equalisation of rates between the richer and poorer boroughs.

October 1924 and the unemployed wait in a long queue outside a labour exchange. Under the 1924 Labour government, partly as a result of Poplar council's campaign, unemployment benefits were increased and more people were made eligible for them.

official opposition and Labour would once more be in third place. Moreover, if Labour turned down this opportunity, this would confirm it as a parliamentary pressure group rather than a party seriously challenging for political power. MacDonald therefore took office, with the intention of demonstrating that the Labour Party could govern competently and establishing it as one of the two major political parties. Beatrice Webb recognised both the benefits and dangers of taking office, when she told her diary: 'For Labour to accept the responsibilities of government is a big risk: it may lead to immediate disaster. But its leaders will become educated in the realities of *political* life and in the work of administration; and even their future behaviour as HMO will be more responsible – more intelligently courteous and bold.'

The desire for the Labour government to be responsible and courteous even extended to the wearing of court dress by cabinet members on ceremonial occasions, which was deeply shocking to the party's class warriors.

Few members of Labour administration had experience of government. In constructing his cabinet, MacDonald went outside the party to fill some offices, including the appointment of former Liberal Lord

Haldane as Lord Chancellor. MacDonald himself became Foreign Secretary as well as Prime Minister. Snowden was Chancellor of the Exchequer, Clynes the Lord Privy Seal, Henderson went to the Home Office and Wheatley to the Ministry of Health. The party's inexperience was also apparent in its approach to the business of government. MacDonald was suspicious of his officials in Downing Street, and insisted on opening all his post himself until it became obvious that this was too impractical. He was also concerned about his income, aware of the fact that he would not be in office for long; all the shopping for Downing Street was bought at a local Co-operative store and delivered in a Co-op van to Number 10.

Even though the party was new to government and had modest objectives, the achievements of this first Labour government should not be underestimated. Without a majority in the House of Commons, MacDonald's administration nevertheless managed to pass legislation on a range of issues. For example, Wheatley's 1924 Housing Act provided government aid to build two and a half million new houses for rent by 1939 – the first large-scale programme for the building of council homes. On education, Trevelyan approved the building of new schools and increased the budget for adult education. On unemployment, which stood at 1.4 million at the beginning of 1924, the cabinet's special unemployment policy committee proposed subsidising electrical development in rural areas and the construction of a national grid, with legislation in this area planned for later in the session. Meanwhile the Insurance Act of 1911 was amended to increase unemployment benefits for men and women, and the criteria for eligibility were extended. Snowden's first budget as Chancellor cut both direct and indirect taxation and was hailed as a victory for working people. Snowden himself described the programme as 'the greatest step ever taken towards the Radical idea of the free breakfast table'.

MacDonald's greatest successes came in foreign policy. By 1924 there was growing

in June 1924 MacDonald (in plus-fours) walks in the garden at Chequers with French premier Herriot (in the pale suit) during the talks on German reparations and French occupation of the Ruhr. MacDonald was Foreign Secretary as well as Prime Minister in the first Labour government, and his greatest successes at this time were in foreign policy.

international tension. Germany had failed to maintain reparation payments, and in return France had occupied the Ruhr, Germany's industrial heartland. The Dawes conference held to resolve the disagreement in April 1924 concluded that Germany had to be made economically stable if reparations were to be paid, and there was implied criticism of the French occupation. France refused to adopt the Dawes plan, however, and MacDonald spent most of his period as Foreign Secretary trying to win the French round. He held talks first with the French and Belgians at Chequers and then hosted an Inter-Allied conference in London in July 1924. His powers of persuasion and shrewd negotiating skills succeeded in getting the French leader Herriot to agree to everything in the Dawes plan except an immediate withdrawal from the Ruhr, and in August fresh agreements on peace and reparations between the allies and Germany were signed in London. It was a real accomplishment for MacDonald. Only three years earlier he had been out of parliament, rejected by the Woolwich electorate for his

In 1924 the call came from the *Workers' Weekly* to men of the armed forces not to shoot strikers. A prosecution for sedition was started, then withdrawn, and the government was suspected of interfering in a legal judgment for political reasons. A Commons defeat on this brought the first Labour administration to an end.

THE FORCES

(Special Service Supplement to the Workers' Weekly)

Vol. I. No. 1.   FRIDAY, AUGUST 1, 1924

SOLDIERS, SAILORS, AIRMEN!
Will You Kill Your Mates?

REMEMBER—YOU ARE WORKERS!
The Bosses are Your Enemies.

DON'T SHOOT STRIKERS! They are workers like you. They are fighting for a decent living for themselves and their women and kids. If the profiteering capitalists, through their agents—your officers—tell you to murder British workers—**DON'T SHOOT.**

THEY ARE GETTING READY	WE APPEAL TO YOU	FORM YOUR OWN COMMITTEES
NEXT WAR ANY TIME NOW	"Join the Army and see the world." Or join the Navy to escape unemployment. Or join the Air Force and get through your apprenticeship without starving. These are the promises and compulsion used to recruit	Your fellow workers have their

anti-war record, but now he was Prime Minister, helping to resolve international disagreements and building the peaceful world in which he so passionately believed.

The evidence also suggests that Labour's record in office was popular with the electorate. In March 1924, Henderson won the Burnley by-election, increasing Labour's majority there, and in May the party took West Toxteth from the Conservatives. Nevertheless, it was far from plain sailing for the government. Labour was dependent on Liberal support to pass legislation and there were many Commons defeats, as with the Rent Restrictions Act. The government was also prone to errors, and it was one such mistake that led to its downfall.

An article in *Workers' Weekly* had called for soldiers in the British army not to turn their guns on fellow workers in industrial disputes. The Attorney-General, Sir Patrick Hastings, believed the article to be seditious and initiated a prosecution of the paper's editor, John Campbell. However there was a good deal of criticism of this decision from the Labour benches, and, although it appears that no political pressure was put on Hastings by the cabinet, his later decision to withdraw the prosecution gave a strong impression that MacDonald's government had interfered in a legal judgement for political reasons. The Conservatives and Liberals joined to defeat the government on the issue, and MacDonald used this as an opportunity to dissolve parliament.

The notorious Zinoviev letter: 'We're sunk'

The question of Anglo-Russian relations was an issue during the entire election campaign and was fuelled by Conservative propaganda. The October 1917 revolution in Russia had sharpened fears of socialist revolution elsewhere; in 1924 under Labour, full recognition of the Soviet government and plans for a loan to Russia led to accusations of links between MacDonald and Lenin and attacks on socialism and communism. In the final week of the campaign the infamous Zinoviev letter was published in the *Daily Mail*. The letter purported to be from Zinoviev, President of the Communist International, and appealed for insurrection and revolution in Britain, calling on the section of the Labour Party sympathetic to communist aims to put pressure on their government. In this atmosphere of fervent anti-communism, and without a clear lead from MacDonald on the authenticity of the letter,

The Zinoviev Letter: A Call to Armed Insurrection?

To the Central Committee, British Communist Party
Dear Comrades,

The time is approaching for the Parliament of England to consider the Treaty concluded between the Governments of Great Britain and the SSSR for the purpose of ratification.

It is indispensible to stir up the masses of the British proletariat to bring into movement the army of unemployed proletarians whose position can be improved only after a loan has been granted to the SSSR....A settlement of relations between the two countries will assist in the revolutionising of the international and British proletariat not less than a successful rising on any of the working districts of England, as the establishment of close contact between the British and Russian proletariat, the exchange of delegations and workers, etc., will make it possible for us to extend and develop the propaganda of ideas of Leninism in England and the Colonies. Armed warfare must be preceded by a struggle against the inclination to compromise which are embedded among the majority of British workmen, against the ideas of evolution and peaceful extermination of capitalism. Only then will it be possible to count upon complete success of an armed insurrection...

Form a directing operative head of the Military Section.

Do not put this off to a future moment, which may be pregnant with events and catch you unprepared.

Desiring you all success, both in organisation and in your struggle.

With Communist Greetings, President of the Presidium of the IKKI

The so-called Zinoviev letter, printed in the *Daily Mail* in the final week of the 1924 election campaign, lost Labour the election.

the issue succeeded in discrediting the Labour government. The letter was subsequently shown to be a forgery, but in election week the *Daily Mail* carried the sensational headline: 'CIVIL WAR PLOT BY SOCIALISTS'.

It is difficult to assess how damaging the Zinoviev letter was. On opening the papers and seeing the headlines, J.H. Thomas famously declared: 'We're sunk.' The election was a decisive victory for the Conservatives who, returning to an anti-protectionist position, won 419 seats. But Labour lost only 40 MPs and its vote actually increased by one million to 5.5 million. The real loser was the Liberal Party. It had fielded

100 fewer candidates than in 1923, its parliamentary representation was reduced to 40 and it obtained only 17.6 per cent of the vote. While Labour's first government was over and MacDonald had been badly beaten by the Conservatives, 1924 was nevertheless in many ways a victory for the Labour leader. By leading a competent if not dynamic Labour government, the Liberal Party had finally been displaced as the second party in British politics, just as MacDonald had hoped.

The experience of the Labour government was not seen in these terms by sections of the party, and its defeat led to a shift to the left both in the Parliamentary Party and in the TUC. The growing criticism of MacDonald's leadership coincided with calls for direct action rather than parliamentary methods. These tendencies were intensified when the government returned Britain to the gold standard in April 1925, thereby plunging British coal exports into crisis. The coal owners, whose product was now uncompetitively priced in the international market, responded by cutting pay and lengthening hours. The miners called for strike action and the crisis came to a head in July 1925. The government was not ready for a confrontation and, in order to buy time, Baldwin intervened to subsidise the industry for a year while a Royal Commission investigated the issue.

'Red Friday', as this moment was known, turned out to be a false dawn for the miners. When the Commission reported in March 1926, it called for reduced rates of pay for workers and no government subsidy for the industry. The miners' strike that followed began on 26 April 1926, and the General Committee of the TUC called a general strike in support. In terms of the number of workers who joined the strike, it was extremely effective in many industries. However, the General Committee was badly organised and unprepared for the scale of the stoppage. There was also confusion about the purpose of the strike. While A.J. Cook, secretary of the National Union of Mineworkers, was arguing that 'the cost of a strike of the miners would mean the end of capitalism', John Thomas, leader of the National Union of Railway Workers, was assuring all

A poster for the 1924 election showed MacDonald broadcasting on the wireless. The war had brought great improvements in radio technology, and in 1922 the British Broadcasting Company was set up as a public service, financed by a annual licence fee of ten shillings.

Hello Everybody !
MACDONALD *Calling*

LABOUR *in* **POWER** *THIS* **TIME**

that he had 'never disguised that in a challenge to the constitution, God help us unless the government won'.

Such confusion helps to explain the failure of the strike. The TUC was concerned from the outset that, while the miners were striking against their bosses, the rest of the workers were striking against the government. As the stoppages took effect, it was clear that their actions amounted to a challenge to a democratically elected government. The members of the General Committee were therefore anxious to negotiate with the government to end the strike. After meeting with Sir Herbert Samuel, chairman of the 1925 Royal Commission, they agreed to proposals that meant an immediate cessation of the dispute and reorganisation of the industry, a subsidy to continue to the end of the month, but wage cuts to be left on the table. This proved to be a fatal error on two counts. Firstly, the miners would not support such proposals and felt they had been betrayed by their union colleagues. And, secondly, having called off the stoppage, the trade union leaders discovered that Baldwin had not committed the government to any measures in the Samuel Memorandum. The strike had been ended without securing any of the TUC's own objectives. The miners remained

In April 1926, the miners went on strike against the threat of longer hours for less pay. The TUC called a general strike in support of their claims. The leaflet opposite was issued by the Bristol General Strike Committee.

During the nine-day General Strike an armoured car (below) escorts a food convoy through Oxford Circus on the way to Hyde Park for distribution. The government was well prepared, had access to the radio (there were no newspapers) and recruited volunteers to run transport and essential services.

Why a General Strike?

Because the organised Trade Union Movement resents the degrading conditions sought to be imposed upon the Miners.

The Government declares that it will only re-open negotiations provided the Miners AGREE BEFORE-HAND to reduced wages or longer hours or both.

THIS IS NOT FAIR.

What are Miners' Wages which the Owners and their friends the Government say must be reduced? Look at these figures :—

			Per day		Per day
Scotland	....	....	Hewers, 9/4	....	Labourers, 6/8
Northumberland	....		„ 10/4	....	„ 7/7
Durham	....	....	„ 9/8	....	„ 7/6
South Wales	....	....	„ 9/9	....	„ 8/0
Yorkshire	....	....	„ 10/7	....	„ 9/6

The Bristol rates are worse than these.

The average week is five shifts. **Forest of Dean** daily wage, **8/11½.** Proposed reduction, **3/11½ per day.**

The Owners demand reductions from the above rates of from **5/-** to **28/-** per week, **and an increased working week of five hours.** Bristol Miners are offered **10¾d. per hour** as basic wage for Hewers.

IS THERE MONEY IN COAL?

The profits of the Coal Industry have been as follow :—

25 years, 1889 to 1913 : **260 Million Pounds sterling.** Capital about £130 Million.
12 years, 1914 to 1925 : **232 Million Pounds sterling.** Capital about £200 Million.

In short, investors received all their money back **twice** in the first 25 years, **and in addition** received rather more than the whole of their money back in dividends in the **second period of 12 years.**

No self-respecting body of workers can accept the conditions offered.

The Government is using all its power and resources to defeat the Miners.

THE MINER DEMANDS a reasonable wage, reasonable hours and a National Agreement. It is the bounden duty of all other workers to see that he gets these terms.

THE WAY OUT.

If the Owners cannot organise their industry in such a way as to provide a living wage then, as coal is vital to British Industry, the State must step in and see that justice is done.

The State must OWN the Coal Industry.

Printed by Voluntary Labour at the Bristol Printers Ltd. (T.U. 44-hr. week, Stratton Street, St. Paul's, and issued by the Bristol General Strike Committee, Kingsley Hall, Old Market Street, Bristol.
Signed—A. V. Despres, Chairman, E. H. Parker, Secretary.

on strike until November, but they were eventually forced back to work, utterly defeated. Having stood by the principle 'Not a penny off the pay, not a minute on the day', they ended up being compelled to accept an increase in hours, wage reductions to pre-1921 levels and the loss of the right to national pay settlements.

The Aftermath of the General Strike

The failure of the General Strike affected the Labour Party in many ways. An immediate effect was the passing of the 1927 Trades Disputes Act, which made general strikes illegal and – even more damagingly – required union members to 'contract in' to the political levy to the Labour Party, a change which substantially reduced party funds right up until the Second World War. Twelve months after the strike, the unions had lost more than 300,000 members and their funds had dropped equally sharply.

Some of the effects on the Labour Party were constructive, however. The failure of direct action reinforced the view that socialism could only be achieved through gradual parliamentary action. The balance of power within the Labour Party returned to the parliamentary leadership. MacDonald had spent the period out of office trying to remedy gaps in policy that had bedevilled the first Labour government. With Snowden, MacDonald led a sub-committee of the National Executive charged with the task of drawing up a draft programme for the next general election. This programme, called *Labour and the Nation*, was put in front of the party conference in October 1928, where it gained widespread approval. It called for public ownership of coal, power, transport, life insurance and land; the extension of the social services; progressive taxation; and measures to tackle unemployment.

The economic historian R.H. Tawney had been closely involved in the drafting of *Labour and the Nation*. Tawney was born in 1880 in India, educated at Rugby and Oxford, and had worked in London's East End at Toynbee Hall before becoming a pioneer of the Workers' Educational Association and a distinguished academic. Like the Fabian G.D.H. Cole, the theorist of self-governing industrial guilds, and Harold Laski, political theorist and inspirational teacher of generations of students at the London School of Economics, Tawney was a key intellectual figure in the development of Labour's thinking. In his books, such as *The Acquisitive Society* (1921) and *Equality* (1931), he argued that social

Freedom for the Pike is Death for the Minnows

Liberty and equality have usually in England been considered antithetic; and, since fraternity has rarely been considered at all, the famous trilogy has been easily dismissed as a hybrid abortion. Equality implies the deliberate acceptance of social restraints upon individual expansion. It involves the prevention of sensational extremes of wealth and power by public action for the public good. If liberty means, therefore, that every individual shall be free, according to his opportunities, to indulge without limit his appetite for either, it is clearly incompatible, not only with economic and social, but with civil and political, equality, which also prevent the strong exploiting to the full the advantages of their strength, and, indeed, with any habit of life save that of the Cyclops. But freedom for the pike is death for the minnows. It is possible that equality is to be contrasted, not with liberty, but only with a particular interpretation of it....

When liberty is construed, realistically, as implying, not merely a minimum of civil and political rights, but securities that the economically weak will not be at the mercy of the economically strong, and that the control of those aspects of economic life by which all are affected will be amenable, in the last resort, to the will of all, a large measure of equality, so far from being inimical to liberty, is essential to it. In conditions which impose co-operative, rather than merely individual, effort, liberty is, in fact, equality in action, in the sense, not that all men perform identical functions or wield the same degree of power, but that all men are equally protected against the abuse of power, and equally entitled to insist that power shall be used, not for personal ends, but for the general advantage.

R.H. Tawney, *Equality*, 1931

and economic inequalities prevented large sections of the population from achieving their full potential, both as human beings and citizens. Equality was necessary for freedom. Tawney's work proved compelling as a statement of the essence of democratic socialism.

Tawney was also closely involved in the practical effort to return Labour to office. The Conservatives faced the electorate in 1929 amid rising unemployment, and Tawney spent the last ten days of the campaign touring with MacDonald. Although the Liberals had relaunched themselves under the leadership of Lloyd George in 1926, they managed to win only 59 seats. The Conservatives won 260, but it was Labour who came out in front, with 37.1 per cent of the vote and 288 seats. For the first time in its history Labour was the largest party in Britain. Again it was MacDonald who went to the king, but this time there was little debate in the party about whether Labour should take office.

Labour back in power: the stock market crash and the crises that followed

The second Labour government began quietly. Henderson was given the post he wanted as Foreign Secretary and Thomas became Lord Privy Seal. George Lansbury, supporter of the suffragettes and one of the Poplar councillors imprisoned in 1921, went to the Office of Works. Rising star Oswald Mosley (formerly a Conservative then an Independent MP) became Chancellor of the Duchy of Lancaster. Margaret Bondfield, former Chair of the TUC's General Council, was Minister of Labour, the first ever woman cabinet minister. Snowden returned to the Treasury.

Despite relinquishing the post of Foreign Secretary, MacDonald still retained a close interest in Anglo-American relations, and in September 1929 left for America to finish discussions on naval disarmament. He received a welcome befitting the first British Prime Minister's visit to the United States, including a full ticker-tape parade in New York. Then, within weeks, the American stock market crashed and precipitated a world-wide financial crisis that was eventually to overwhelm MacDonald's government.

The economic crisis was felt at home in the form of rapidly rising unemployment. By January 1930 this stood at one and a half million. Despite criticism to the contrary, the government was not passive in the face of this growing problem. MacDonald created an Economic Advisory Council, including such experts on the economy and industrial matters

Workmen arrived with their spades and pickaxes (opposite, above) at this Bermondsey polling booth during the general election of May 1929. The Labour Party polled the majority of votes for the first time in its history.

The 'flappers' – modern young women in their twenties – were able to vote in the 1929 election (opposite, below). In 1928 all women aged twenty-one and over were enfranchised, with the result that women made up just over half the electorate.

as Cole and Tawney. Also included was John Maynard Keynes, the Cambridge economist and pioneer of the theory of stimulating employment and the circulation of money through government investment in public works. Following its manifesto commitment, Labour initiated a structural reorganisation of large industries such as coal, iron and cotton in an effort to make them more competitive. In June 1930 the government put more money into public works, such as the building of trunk roads and in July the conditions required by local authorities to obtain grants were liberalised. Yet, while the total value of government spending on public works was not negligible, its impact on unemployment was.

In June 1929 Labour was in power again. This photograph of the cabinet at 10 Downing Street includes Ramsay MacDonald, Arthur Henderson, Sidney Webb, (from left to right in the front row) and Arthur Greenwood, Minister for Health (back row centre).

Spending doubled in 1930, but without bringing jobs in its wake. By June 1930 unemployment had reached almost two million, and it topped two and a half million in December.

The growing economic crisis sparked off a political crisis within the Labour Party. In January 1930, Oswald Mosley sent a memorandum to MacDonald on the economic situation asking for more radical measures to deal with the high unemployment levels, including an overhaul of the machinery of government, massive government investment in public works, and a new economic department to look at longer-term economic reconstruction. MacDonald is said to have been sympathetic to some of Mosley's plans, but they were ruled out by Snowden and other members of the cabinet. In May 1930 Mosley resigned in frustration from the cabinet and in 1931 was expelled from the party altogether when he formed the New Party, a party of 'vitality and manhood', declared a proscribed organisation by Labour and later renamed the British Union of Fascists.

Another line of attack came from the Independent Labour Party. The ILP had gradually become separated in aims and objectives from the main body of the Labour Party and in 1927 it had put forward its own document *Socialism in our Time*. Critical of the Labour leadership, it put pressure on its sponsored MPs to follow its own line and not that of the party. The divisions became too much for the relationship and in 1932 the ILP disaffiliated from Labour.

Meanwhile unemployment had ceased to be simply a social and industrial issue and had become a matter of financial confidence. The 1924 Labour government's increases in the amount paid to the unemployed meant that now the bill for unemployment benefits was alarmingly high. The numbers of jobless also substantially reduced the amount of taxes collected by the Treasury. These two factors led to a massive budget deficit. MacDonald was not unaware of these pressures, but, except for a cabinet reshuffle, there was little response from his government. This lack of action has often led commentators to one of two conclusions. On the one hand, the lack of decisive leadership from MacDonald has been blamed for the failure of the government to respond positively to the crisis. On the other hand, the Labour Party has itself been blamed, on the grounds that its ideology was insufficiently practical and that this made it unprepared for such a financial situation.

Neither argument is wholly persuasive. It was true that MacDonald spent much time preoccupied with foreign policy, but he saw the international crisis and the economic crisis at home as inextricably linked. Without a strong European market, Britain would have no export industry and little hope of solving the problem of unemployment.

There was also evidence that it was not MacDonald who was indecisive and unable to make decisions, but his cabinet. In the difficult circumstances that it faced, there were three possible options. The cabinet could cut unemployment benefit and reduce the budget deficit through deflationary measures; it could invest massively in public works to reduce the number of people unemployed and lift tax revenues; or it could protect the home markets by imposing a tariff on imports to Britain. The first option was advocated strongly by Snowden, and to a lesser degree by MacDonald, but was strongly opposed by Henderson and other cabinet members. The second course had been advocated by Mosley and Keynes, and MacDonald also toyed with the idea in some form, but it was too radical for an inexperienced Labour government that wanted to build a reputation for orthodoxy (later this course was followed under Roosevelt's administration in the USA – the 'New Deal'). The third option, the imposition of protective tariffs, found few friends and was dismissed. The cabinet was presented with several solutions to the problem, but it failed to follow any of them.

The financial crisis came to a head in the summer of 1931 with the collapse of the Austrian bank, Credit Anstalt. This led to a loss of confidence in the international money markets and, with a massive budget deficit, there was a drain on British gold reserves. But MacDonald was effectively immobilised. The cabinet would not agree to large cuts in unemployment benefits and called instead for tax rises. In order to get such proposals through the Commons, Labour needed the support of either the Liberals or Tories who both wanted smaller tax rises and greater benefit cuts. Eventually, after days of discussion and much lobbying by MacDonald, the cabinet voted on the proposals. A majority was in favour of benefit cuts, but with Henderson and others prepared to resign over the matter, the government was split and fell.

'I have changed none of my ideals. I have a national duty': broadcast by Ramsay MacDonald, August 1931

At this point, according to David Marquand's biography of MacDonald, the Labour leader intended to resign with his cabinet colleagues and return to the opposition benches. But this was not how the story ended, for when he went to King George V to tender the resignations, MacDonald was told 'he was the only man to lead the country through the crisis and [the King] hoped he would reconsider the situation'. The thoughts of MacDonald during the next few hours are uncertain, but when he met the Labour cabinet for the last time, he announced that he was to lead a National government with Liberal and Conservative support in order to deal with the economic crisis.

After almost a decade as its leader, MacDonald had turned his back on the Labour Party. This was seen as a betrayal and entered the party's culture as a warning of the frailties of leaders. But worse than losing its leader, the party had lost its direction and spirit. The 1929-31 government had failed to deal with unemployment and left office discredited with the nation. At the 1931 elections the official Labour Party was reduced to only 52 seats. It was the party's darkest hour. Not only had its seemingly inexorable advance been halted, but it was far from certain that it could ever recover.

An election poster of October 1931 (opposite) for MacDonald's National government attacking socialist promises. MacDonald had been expelled from the Labour party in the previous month.

The National coalition was ridiculed in *Punch* (below): 'Wi' MacDonald, Sir Donald, Sam (Herbert), Sam Hoare, Jim Thomas, Stan' Baldwin, old Uncle Phil Snowden and all.' The old grey mare died in the original version of the old song 'Widdicombe Fair'.

SOCIALIST PROMISES WEIGHED AND FOUND WANTING

UNEMPLOYMENT — BAD TRADE — LESS WAGES

VOTE FOR THE NATIONAL GOVERNMENT

KITCHEN.

"PUBLISHED BY THE NATIONAL UNION OF CONSERVATIVE AND UNIONIST ASSOCIATIONS, PALACE CHAMBERS, WESTMINSTER, S.W.1. AND PRINTED BY JAMES COND, LTD., GREAT CHARLES STREET, BIRMINGHAM."

C 315

Chapter Three
From Defeat to War
1931–1945

Ramsay MacDonald's decision to form a National government meant that he was immediately shunned by the Labour Party. What was seen as his act of betrayal ensured his expulsion from the party in September 1931, along with Snowden, Thomas and others, who then formed the National Labour Group. But the feelings of resentment and betrayal were felt on both sides. Snowden blamed his Labour colleagues for preventing a cabinet response to the crisis and warned Labour members on the eve of the general election that 'only a few weeks, possibly, remain before the place that knows them now will know them no more'. During the election campaign, Snowden stepped up his attacks, describing the 1931 Labour manifesto as 'Bolshevism run mad'.

Whatever the interpretations of the 1931 crisis, it had a number of immediate effects on the Labour Party. The first and most disastrous was the result of the 1931 general election. In September, Britain was forced off the gold standard to stop speculation against the pound, an option that the Labour government never thought it had, and in October the National government under MacDonald introduced the budget which the Labour cabinet had rejected. It then went to the country, asking for a 'doctor's mandate' – a blank cheque for the emergency treatment of the economy. The second Labour government had ended in division and disarray, but there was still no expectation of the electoral disaster that was to follow. When the results were announced, Labour had been reduced from 288 seats to just 52. Nearly all the party's leading lights were defeated, leaving only three former cabinet ministers in the Parliamentary Labour Party: Henderson, Lansbury and the MP for Limehouse, Clement Attlee. Henderson was elected as leader in MacDonald's stead, but at sixty-eight he was past his political prime.

Another effect of the crisis was the growing division between the small Parliamentary Labour Party and the party organisations outside

George Lansbury replaced Henderson in 1932 as leader of the Labour Party in opposition. A leading activist in the Poplar crusade for the working-class unemployed in the 1920s, he continued to speak for them in the depression of the 1930s. He is pictured opposite at an anti-means test rally in Trafalgar Square in August 1936.

parliament. The PLP was dominated by George Lansbury who replaced the ailing Henderson in 1932 and Stafford Cripps, nephew to Beatrice Webb, a brilliant Oxford chemistry graduate who had also made a great deal of money as a patent lawyer. Both were on the left, Lansbury a religious pacifist and Cripps a High Anglican neo-Marxist.

Labour's new generation

Power was now increasingly located outside the Commons, specifically in Transport House, where Labour's up-and-coming generation planned the party's renewal. One of these was Ernest ('Ernie') Bevin, the robustly down-to-earth leader of the Transport and General Workers Union. Bevin, from a very poor West Country background and with little formal education, had formidable political and industrial skills which he used to the full to try to improve the lot of the working class. Initially this meant supporting the class struggle in industry and Bevin had played a major role in the organisation of the General Strike, but 1926 was a turning-point for him, as for others. After the failure of the General Strike, he increasingly recognised the importance of parliamentary methods in achieving his political goals.

Another man making his mark was Hugh Dalton. Dalton was educated at Eton, Cambridge and the LSE where he went on to teach economics and where he cultivated the political growth of such promising young economists as Hugh Gaitskell and Evan Durbin. Dalton had an enormous physique and a personality to match. This ensured that he aroused considerable antipathy, but to his friends he was affectionately known as Big Hugh and the energy and intellectual effort which he devoted to the Labour Party earned him the nickname of 'Dr Dynamo'.

Bevin and Dalton spearheaded the attempt to renew the Labour Party, Bevin as the practical organiser and Dalton as the intellectual force. The 1930s threw up important challenges for the party. There were increasing tensions and darkening shadows in international relations after Adolf Hitler came to power in Germany in 1933, and it was becoming clear to many that the 1914–18 conflict had not after all been 'the war to end all wars'. Yet the PLP under George Lansbury was completely opposed to the use of military force. This stance was supported by many of the rank and file, and was clearly reflected at the 1933 conference in the passing of a motion calling for a general strike against war.

Bevin and Dalton felt that there were intellectual and political shortcomings in such a position, and they started a determined campaign to change it. Cripps was forced to resign from the National Council of Labour on its commitment to strong sanctions against Italy following Mussolini's invasion of Abyssinia in 1935. Then at the 1935 party conference, Bevin ridiculed Lansbury's position on the same issue, accusing him of 'hawking your conscience around from body to body asking to be told what you ought to do with it'. The conference overwhelmingly backed the decision of the National Council on rearmament and Lansbury resigned. Told by a colleague that he had been too hard on Lansbury, Bevin replied viciously: 'Lansbury has been going about dressed up in saint's clothes for years waiting for martyrdom. I set fire to the faggots.'

Clement Attlee was the main beneficiary of Lansbury's resignation. Attlee had held office in both the 1924 and 1929 Labour governments, though without making a great impression in either. His style was reserved and cautious, in complete contrast to Dalton and Bevin. But

In the general election of 1935 Manny Shinwell stood against MacDonald, Labour's former leader, in the Durham constituency of Seaham Harbour. Shinwell won a resounding victory for Labour with a 20,000 majority. MacDonald felt like a drowning man in these last years of his life: 'Sinks below surface…and becomes vaguer and dimmer and is at last lost.'

with talent in short supply in the Parliamentary Party in the early 1930s, Attlee was able to build up his standing as deputy leader. When Lansbury resigned just before the 1935 election, it was Clem Attlee who stepped into his shoes, albeit on a temporary basis.

The 1935 general election saw the partial recovery of Labour. The party won 154 seats and included in the numbers were leading figures such as Dalton, Morrison and Shinwell. Herbert Morrison had proved himself as a highly energetic administrator and political organiser as the Leader of London County Council, which Labour had dramatically snatched from the Tories for the first time in the 1934 local elections. Emanuel ('Manny') Shinwell, in 1921 a fiery working-class activist in Clydeside, had defeated Ramsay MacDonald in a bitter contest for Seaham Harbour in Durham; MacDonald died two years later, an outcast and a broken man. The Labour Party lost another former leader in 1935, with the death of Arthur Henderson. After the election, there was a ballot for the Labour leadership, this time between Attlee, Morrison and Arthur Greenwood, Minister of Health in Labour's two minority

Thousands thronged the streets in October 1936 to prevent the black-shirted supporters of Oswald Mosley from marching through working-class districts of the East End of London. Cable Street (below) was the scene of the fiercest anti-fascist battle; demonstrators carrying missiles flee as the police break down their barricade.

administrations. Dalton backed Morrison, who was widely expected to win, but when there was no victory on the first ballot, Attlee gained most of Greenwood's second votes and was elected.

The late thirties were turbulent years, both at home and abroad. The death of King George V in 1936 was followed ten months later by the shock over the abdication of King Edward VIII and his controversial marriage to American divorcee Mrs Simpson. Britain also faced the persistent problem of high unemployment, a difficult issue for Labour. The party was acutely aware that under MacDonald it had failed to get to grips with soaring unemployment, which at one point reached over three million. The hardship that unemployment brought was made worse by the hated household 'means test' which took into account the income of whole families, including pensions for the old and the pay packets of any working children. The historic Jarrow March of 1936 was only one of several 'hunger marches' and marches for jobs in the 1930s. Ellen Wilkinson ('Red Ellen'), the tough and charismatic MP for the Tyneside shipbuilding constituency of Jarrow, marched with her constituents as they walked to London with their petition for jobs.

The world-wide depression of the 1930s destroyed international trade and unemployment in Britain was highest in the industries and the regions that had lost their export markets, such as iron and steel, shipbuilding and cotton manufacture. Among the regions of high unemployment was Lancashire; the faces of these men outside the Wigan labour exchange show their resignation.

The Jarrow marchers reached Luton, led by MP Ellen Wilkinson, in a rare burst of sunshine (above); most of the way they wore their groundsheets as rain capes. With unemployment of over 75 per cent, Jarrow felt itself a murdered town. This dignified march for jobs in October 1936 was met with deep respect, except in parliament where their MP was given three minutes to speak before the House moved on to other business.

The Labour Party's programme for planning and support for rearmament

In response to the problem of unemployment, Labour's National Executive set up a number of specific policy committees, many of which were chaired by Dalton. His experience of the 1931 economic crisis, together with his observation of the relative economic successes in Germany, Italy and Russia, made Dalton a keen supporter of planning. Although he was not a disciple of Keynesian economics, the influence of which was spreading after the publication of Keynes's *The General Theory of Employment, Interest and Money* in 1936, Dalton was sympathetic to the idea of deficit budgeting, and Keynesian ideas were gradually incorporated into Labour Party policy.

But the most concrete expression of the discussions on planning was Labour's *Immediate Programme*, published in 1937. Written by Dalton, this programme was, as its title suggests, an attempt to provide practical economic policies for a Labour government. There were proposals for an increase in pensions and a better health service, the establishment of a National Investment Board which would advise on employment policies, and plans for housing, electrification and transport. It showed Dalton's attachment to planning and the control of the levers of the economy. The document proposed nationalisation of the key industries, including coal, transport, electricity, gas and armaments. But it also advanced policies designed to extend Labour's appeal beyond the working class, and to win middle-class voters.

International relations and defence were also matters of grave concern. In 1936 Germany repudiated post-war treaties and remilitarised the Rhineland. That same year the Spanish Civil War became a stage for rival ideologies – Germany and Italy supplied men and arms to Franco's right-wing insurgents, Soviet advisers and equipment and thousands of European volunteers supported the Popular Front government.

Within Labour's ranks, the struggle to reform its defence policy continued. In 1936 Labour was still opposed to general rearmament, and consistently voted against the annual service estimates in the Commons. As Foreign Affairs spokesman, Dalton used his formidable energies and powers of persuasion to get the Parliamentary Party to abstain from the vote in 1937. This was taken further at the next party conference, which endorsed a statement drafted by Dalton opposing appeasement and supporting proposals to rebuild British armaments. This position was denounced by Stafford Cripps, who called for a Popular Front with Liberals, Communists and the ILP to oppose fascism, but in 1937, the Socialist League which was led by Cripps disaffiliated from the Labour Party and Cripps himself was expelled in 1939.

With the Labour Party committed to rearmament after 1937, there was increasing opposition to Neville Chamberlain's policy of appeasement. In 1938, to avoid a German invasion of Czechoslovakia, Prime Minister Chamberlain signed the agreement with Hitler in Munich conceding Czech territory to Germany to guarantee 'peace in our time'.
Yet Chamberlain's failure to initiate full-scale rearmament and the unravelling of his settlement with Hitler led to criticism from both Conservative backbenchers and the Labour leadership, but, with only 167 seats in the Commons against Chamberlain's 418, Labour could do little to influence government policy in September 1939.

Neville Chamberlain was the target of this tableau at the biggest ever socialist May Day Rally in 1938. His policy of appeasement had allowed Hitler to annexe Austria in March and to plan further German expansion. The ideologies of socialism and fascism became increasingly polarised in the 1930s.

War became inevitable when German troops invaded Poland on 1 September 1939. The British and French had guaranteed Poland against aggression after Czechoslovakia had been overrun by Hitler. So began the second world conflict in the space of a generation. Labour was immediately invited to join the government, but refused to do so while Chamberlain remained at its head, though it did enter an electoral arrangement which meant that by-elections would not be contested. And discontent on the Tory benches at Chamberlain's handling of the crisis was mounting, already evident when Leo Amery shouted across to Arthur Greenwood, about to speak in the Commons on the eve of war, 'Speak for England, Arthur.'

In 1940 the political crisis reached a head with the failure of the British expeditionary forces in Norway. In the subsequent vote in the Commons, Labour united with 40 Tory dissidents to reduce the government majority to 81, a clear vote of no confidence in Chamberlain's leadership. But Chamberlain clung to power, appealing again to the Labour leadership to enter the government. There was much debate within the National Executive Committee about whether Labour should accept, but eventually Attlee reported the party's decision. Labour would serve in a coalition, but not one headed by the current prime minister. With this response Chamberlain tendered his resignation, his policy of appeasement in tatters and his reputation as prime minister stained by his failure to rearm Britain. He was one of the 'Guilty Men' who were widely blamed for leaving Britain unprepared for war.

Pulling together in wartime: the coalition government

Britain's new war leader achieved a standing in the country in complete contrast to that of Chamberlain. But Prime Minister Winston Churchill – soon to be famous for his ringing war speeches, his cigars and 'V for victory' sign – could not prosecute the war alone. He headed a coalition government, with Labour's Attlee and Greenwood brought into the war cabinet. Churchill recognised the importance of winning the support of the unions, and so took the unusual step of bringing Bevin into the government as Minister for Labour, despite the fact that he was not an MP. Bevin was quickly found a seat, in Central Wandsworth, where he was returned in a by-election later in 1940. Dalton was also appointed to a key post in the Ministry for Economic Warfare.

Almost the first decision Churchill faced was the preservation of the British army by the withdrawal of British troops from the beaches of Dunkirk in June 1940. The toughest part of the conflict was from June 1940 right through 1941. Italy entered the war on Germany's side after German troops had overrun the Netherlands, Belgium and northern France and the French government had sued for peace. The Soviet Union had signed a non-aggression pact with Germany in 1939, prior to the Nazi-Soviet dismemberment of Poland. Britain now stood alone fighting Germany. The Royal Air Force won the Battle of Britain in August and September 1940, but in the autumn German aircraft returned to the British skies at night to blitz London and other major cities. On the night of 10 May 1941 the chamber of the House of Commons was itself destroyed by a bomb, forcing a temporary move along the corridor to the House of Lords. It was not until June 1941, when Hitler abandoned the pact with Stalin and invaded Russia, that the British people on the home front experienced a break in the German onslaught. The campaign on the Eastern Front cost Hitler very dear, and also changed the general British attitude to the Soviet Union, now seen as a stalwart ally in the war to free Europe. December 1941 also brought

This David Low cartoon of May 1940 conveys the new determination and energy that Churchill's coalition government inspired in a whole nation at war. Churchill, Attlee, Bevin, Morrison and Amery lead the way, rolling up their sleeves for action.

ALL BEHIND YOU, WINSTON

the entry of the USA into the war, following the surprise Japanese bombing of the US Pacific fleet in Pearl Harbour.

The Second World War had a profound impact on British society and on its politics. Labour was to be a direct beneficiary of this. Rationing, national conscription, the blitz, women workers in the factories and on the land and the evacuation of hundreds of thousands of children from the town to safety in the country – the demands and necessities of war served to bring people together from many different areas and backgrounds in a common cause. Moreover, the war effort was sustainable only if people felt that post-war Britain would not return to the unemployment and economic misery of the 1930s, a point that Labour leaders lost no opportunity to emphasise.

Then there was the changing role of government itself. War demanded greater state control of many areas of economic and social life. As a result of the blitz, the fire services were amalgamated into a National Fire Service, while improvements in health care were made through the Emergency Medical Services. At Attlee's behest the coalition government agreed to subsidise milk for children under five and

Ernest Bevin, from 1921 the powerful general secretary of the huge Transport and General Workers' Union, was Minister for Labour in Churchill's government. The poster opposite was part of his export drive.

The war was a great leveller. Food rationing, introduced in 1940, and queues for most goods (below) became a part of life.

A Ministry of Labour recruiting poster (below right) calls for women factory workers to help the war effort.

ERNEST BEVIN

SAYS –

"We must have Exports"

IF YOU ARE WORKING FOR

EXPORT

YOU ARE WORKING FOR

VICTORY

ISSUED BY THE EXPORT COUNCIL BOARD OF TRADE. AUGUST 1940

A Time for Revolutions, Not for Patching

In proceeding from this first comprehensive survey of social insurance to the next task – of making recommendations – three guiding principles may be laid down at the outset.

The first principle is that any proposals for the future, while they should use to the full the experience gathered in the past, should not be restricted by consideration of sectional interests established in the obtaining of that experience. Now, when the war is abolishing landmarks of every kind, is the opportunity for using experience in a clear field. A revolutionary moment in the world's history is a time for revolutions, not for patching.

The second principle is that organisation of social insurance should be treated as one part only of a comprehensive policy of social progress. Social insurance fully developed may provide income security; it is an attack upon Want. But Want is one only of five giants of the road to reconstruction and in some ways the easiest to attack. The others are Disease, Ignorance, Squalor and Idleness.

The third principle is that social security must be achieved by co-operation between the State and the individual. The State should offer security for service and contribution. The State in organising security should not stifle incentive, opportunity, responsibility; in establishing a national minimum, it should leave room and encouragement for voluntary action by each individual to provide more than that minimum for himself and his family. *The Beveridge Report, 1942*

Sir William Beveridge addresses a meeting (above) of MPs, peers, journalists and social workers. Many were members of the Social Security League, founded to press for the reform of the social services proposed in the Beveridge Report of 1942. The packed meeting was chaired by Barbara Wootton.

their mothers. The Town and Country Planning Act in 1944 extended the role of the state in local matters.

One of the most significant areas of state activity was in employment policy. Under the eye of Ernest Bevin, the government was able to maintain a high level of production by planning the use of its limited skilled workforce. In return for the co-operation of the workforce, Bevin made improvements to working conditions, including the introduction of employers' liability for the welfare of their workers, and establishing nursery schools to enable women to work in the factories. While the war was on, unemployment in Britain virtually disappeared.

In fact the war had seen the adoption of almost all the key planning measures that Labour had advocated in peace time. Together with proposals from the Liberal Sir William Beveridge (Director of the LSE 1919–37) to reform the social services and the Conservative R.A. ('Rab') Butler to reform the education system, the changing role of the state during the war produced a significant shift to the left in public opinion. A report of the Mass Observation Unit stated that, by December 1942, two out of five people had changed their political outlook.

It was not until 1944 that the war turned decisively in the allies' favour. On 6 June, D-Day, huge numbers of British and American troops landed on the Normandy beaches, and fought their way south, pushing German forces back and liberating first Paris and then almost the whole of France. Germany responded with the launch of its new secret weapon, the V-1 or 'buzzbomb'; these were fired from German territory and fell randomly across London. But with allied forces crossing the Rhine in March 1945 and Russian forces beating back the German offensive from the east, Germany was overrun and finally defeated in May 1945. In September 1945 victory over Japan was also celebrated. In August the first atomic bombs, developed in collaboration by American and British scientists, had been exploded over Hiroshima and Nagasaki, their mushroom clouds a sinister image for the nuclear era.

The end of the war in Europe had also brought an end to the coalition in Britain. Churchill remained at the head of a caretaker government until the result of the general election in July 1945, a result which was delayed by three weeks to enable the counting of the armed forces' vote. The election campaign was relatively peaceful, reflecting the close relationship of the leading figures during the war, notwithstanding Churchill's infamous charge that a socialist government would inevitably need the creation of a Gestapo to suppress freedom of expression. There was also some confusion about who was really running the Labour Party, caused by outspoken party chairman Harold Laski. Attlee had agreed to accompany Churchill to the Potsdam conference of allied powers, but Laski declared that the Labour Party would not be bound by any decisions made by its leader in Potsdam. Churchill sought to exploit this, claiming it was not clear who made the decisions in the Labour Party, but Attlee's characteristically terse note to Laski ('a period of silence on your part would be welcome') served to make it clear enough.

The Labour manifesto, *Let us Face the Future*, struck a chord with the public when

Major Denis Healey, still in his army uniform, was a speaker at the Labour Party conference in June 1945 as Labour made its plans for power in peacetime. The war in Europe had ended only the month before.

The film title *To Have and Have Not* resonates with the Labour poster for the election campaign of 1945, promising a good home for every family. After the hardships of war there was a general feeling that the British people should continue to pull together for a fairer future.

it declared: 'Victory in war must be followed by a prosperous peace'. It called for widespread nationalisation, including coal, electricity and the Bank of England, as well as a bold house-building programme, the creation of a National Health Service and the implementation of Beveridge's social insurance scheme. Labour pledged itself to build a new Britain, dispelling the 'five giant evils' of want, squalor, disease, ignorance and unemployment.

Chapter Four
Building a New World
1945–1951

The result of the 1945 General Election was a landslide to Labour. The party won almost 48 per cent of the vote and 393 seats in the Commons, gaining a huge majority over Churchill. The Conservatives, who had gone into the war with 418 MPs, lost no less than 200 of these, ending up with only 213 MPs. The Liberals also did badly, winning 9 per cent of the vote and 12 seats. It was Labour's finest hour.

Yet the result was a surprise both inside and outside the Labour Party. Attlee later admitted in his memoirs that he was expecting to lose the 1945 election. Churchill himself appeared similarly perplexed. To his wife, who consolingly said the election loss was a blessing in disguise, Churchill replied: 'At the moment it seems quite effectively disguised'.

One thing was clear: Labour had for the first time in its history won a decisive mandate from the electorate. The result meant that Labour was not dependent on the support of other parties to pass its programme, as it had been in its other two periods in office. In addition, unlike 1924 and 1929, Labour's cabinet included people who had already experienced office in the war coalition. When Clement Attlee went to Buckingham Palace to accept office from the king, driven by his wife in their little family car, it was as the leader of an explicitly socialist party who had been given clear approval by the British people for radical national change. It was a vote for a better future and for a rejection of a discredited past of dole queues and means tests. Labour's destiny – and responsibility – was to build the post-war world.

Attlee's appointments to his cabinet were in many ways determined by the personal rivalries that occupied his key colleagues. Ernest Bevin was initially his first choice for Chancellor and Hugh Dalton for Foreign Secretary, but the two were swapped around to keep Bevin further away from his arch-rival Herbert Morrison. Morrison had been actively involved in an abortive attempt to replace Attlee immediately after the

Labour celebrates its huge victory (opposite) in the 1945 election. Bevin, Foreign Secretary in Attlee's government, stands far right. Just behind the leader is Bevin's rival Morrison, whose skilful management of the Commons was to be invaluable for the new administration's full programme of reform legislation.

Labour's Landslide Our talks were interrupted in order that we might return home to hear the result of the General Election....During the count rumours of Labour victories began to come in. We drove through the City and picked up at Waterloo my daughter Alison, who was returning from school, and went on to Transport House. There seemed to be much excitement outside and crowds of photographers. We were greeted with great enthusiasm and found that there was every indication of a landslide in our favour. Conservative Ministers were losing seats and we were making a clean sweep of the big towns. As the day wore on, country results confirmed our victory and by the middle of the afternoon it was clear that we had won a great victory. Clement Attlee, *As It Happened* (on the 1945 election result)

The first photograph taken of the Labour cabinet of 1945 includes Cripps, Greenwood, Bevin, Attlee, Morrison, Dalton (third to eighth, left to right) in the front row with Ellen Wilkinson on the end. Bevan is on the extreme left of the back row and Shinwell third from right.

election success, a manoeuvre which angered Attlee. On hearing of this challenge to his leadership, he called Morrison and told him: 'If you go on mucking about like this, you won't be in the bloody government at all'. In the end Morrison was relegated to the position of Lord President, in charge of the running of the Commons but without a departmental brief. It was a team of large and often conflicting personalities but with formidable collective talent.

Another of Bevin's rivals was Aneurin ('Nye') Bevan. Bevan was born in South Wales, the son of a miner, and he himself worked down the pits at the age of fourteen. His political beliefs were informed by a version of Marxism and after his election to the House of Commons in 1929 Bevan came to represent the voice of the left wing of the party. He was out of the party for a brief period in the late 1930s, expelled for his open support of the Popular Front, yet a few years later he was a member of Attlee's cabinet, responsible for creating a National Health Service, as well as holding the post of Minister for Housing. However, his political views were such that he was widely disliked by many of his more moderate colleagues, especially Bevin. Told on one occasion that Nye was his own worst enemy, Ernest Bevin replied, 'Not while I'm alive, he ain't.'

There was also a place in the cabinet as President of the Board of Trade for Stafford Cripps, who along with Bevan had been expelled from the party in 1939. Then there was Ellen Wilkinson, who became Minister for Education. The 1945 election saw many more women standing and being elected for parliament. There were 87 women candidates, the greatest number ever, over half of whom were Labour. Of the 24 women elected, all but 3 were Labour MPs.

The peaceful revolution: setting up the welfare state

With his team in place, Attlee quickly set about turning the ambitious 1945 election manifesto, *Let us Face the Future* into a programme of legislation. The newly elected Labour MP John Freeman summed up the feelings of many when, in his first speech in the Commons: 'We have before us a battle for peace, no less arduous and no less momentous than the battle we have lived through in the last six years. Today the strategy begins to unfold itself. Today we go into action. Today may rightly be regarded as D-Day in the Battle of the New Britain.' The excitement was too much for the other Labour members who, when first assembled together on the government's benches, broke out in an impromptu rendition of 'The Red Flag'.

The government's first King's Speech in 1945 set the reforming tone for its whole period in office, including proposals for the nationalisation of the Bank of England, coal and civil aviation, all of which went through without much criticism from the Conservative Opposition. These were followed by the nationalisation of cables and wireless and

Nye Bevan, Minister for Housing, declares open the five-hundredth permanent post-war house in Elstree. One of Labour's election promises had been to provide a good home for every family, but at first shortages of materials and manpower were a problem for Bevan.

THIS COLLIERY IS NOW
MANAGED BY THE
NATIONAL
COAL BOARD
ON BEHALF OF THE PEOPLE
JANUARY 1ST 1947

electricity in 1947, and transport and gas in 1948. The only aspect of Labour's public ownership policy which caused any real controversy was its proposal to nationalise the iron and steel industries. The two were both profitable private industries and the government faced defeat on the Iron and Steel Bill by the Conservative majority in the House of Lords. The Labour administration reacted to this firstly by passing an Act of Parliament further restricting the delaying powers of the Lords from two years to one, and secondly by setting the vesting date for iron and steel for February 1951, after a general election, which would allow them to obtain a mandate to enact the proposals. However the delay also gave the owners of the companies the opportunity to lobby the public over the issue, an opportunity which they fully exploited.

Also included in the 1945 King's Speech were Labour's proposals to build a welfare state. As we have seen, even before the outbreak of war and publication of the Beveridge Report, the party was committed to the establishment of a national health service and a system of social security. In government, Labour passed the National Insurance Act of 1946, creating a national contributory insurance scheme which offered unemployment, retirement, sickness and other benefits. And under the leadership of Nye Bevan, the National Health Service legislation was passed in 1946. This bill, opposed by Churchill and the British Medical Association, created a 'comprehensive health service designed to secure the improvement in the physical and mental health of the people' and

The announcement of its nationalisation is unveiled at Murton colliery in Durham in 1947. Manny Shinwell, Minister for Fuel, and Lord Hindley, Chairman of the National Coal Board, raise their hats in salute as socialist principle is put into practice

Nye Bevan's appointment as Minister for Health was not welcomed by the British Medical Association. In Vicky's 1947 cartoon (below), doctors in private practice in Harley Street lie in ambush as Bevan brings plans for 'free health for all'.

HERE HE COMES, BOYS !

Foreign Secretary Ernest Bevin, reads a brief for the 1946 Paris Peace Conference. This working-class minister – down-to-earth, decisive and with a great capacity for hard work – inspired an unusually deep respect and affection in his civil servants, especially at the Foreign Office.

one which was largely free. There were three tiers to the service, with GPs providing primary care, local authorities facilitating health and welfare services and nationalised hospitals providing hospital care. Funding for the service came in part from National Insurance contributions and in the main from central government taxation. The NHS was to be Labour's greatest and most valued achievement.

In fact, the Labour government passed an act of legislation for almost every single pledge contained in *Let us Face the Future*. It is a measure of the success of the post-war Labour government that, despite initially opposing much of its legislation, by 1950 the Conservative Party had been forced to accept it. Indeed, the agenda of full employment and welfare provision was the basis for a political consensus that was forged by Attlee's government and remained unbroken for a whole post-war generation. As Clement Attlee reflected in the 1950s, under his government Britain had witnessed a 'peaceful revolution'.

However on the economic front, the government had a much more difficult time. When the war ended, Britain was heavily in debt and its domestic economy was structured almost entirely for war production. And as soon as the conflict ended the only life-line for Britain, in the shape of US Lend-Lease, was abruptly stopped. American economists underestimated the economic problems Britain faced, and also wanted to establish the USA as the dominant world economic power. The economist Lord Keynes was immediately dispatched to the USA to negotiate a loan on favourable terms, but the American negotiators were not sympathetic to Britain and agreed to a loan only if Attlee's government made sterling freely convertible and abandoned the system of imperial preferences that allowed Britain special access to certain world markets.

There was much opposition to these terms in Britain. There was a strong feeling that Britain had led the fight against Hitler, but was now being punished by the USA for its war effort. Moreover, the American desire for free world trade appeared somewhat hypocritical when they refused to lower their high protective tariffs. Yet it was clear the country had little option but to accept the loan. Britain was, in Keynes's phrase, facing 'financial Dunkirk' and it desperately needed financial support, no matter how unfavourable the terms.

Austerity: loans, rationing, budgets, then a bonfire of controls

Britain's impoverished financial position inevitably brought with it a number of consequences. Firstly, it meant that – even though the war had ended – policies of austerity were extended. In August 1945 the government announced a cut in petrol rations and food imports; and, having survived the war without it, the country had to cope with bread-rationing from 1946. Secondly, the fragility of the British economic position was made fully clear when sterling convertibility was restored in July 1947. By then the US loan had been almost exhausted, but there had been no substantial revival in British exports. There was an immediate run on the pound which forced Dalton to suspend convertibility only a month after it had been reinstated. Further austerity measures were therefore necessary, including another cut in the petrol ration and a request for an extra half-hour's work from miners.

The debacle over sterling convertibility also led to a political crisis within Labour's leadership. In July 1947, Cripps and Dalton sought to replace Attlee with Bevin. The motivation for a change at the top was in part ideological. Cripps and Dalton wanted more implementation of Keynesian fiscal measures in running the economy and less reliance on physical controls. But their purpose was also to restore direction. They believed that the party was drifting, and that Attlee could not offer the necessary strong leadership. But Bevin was too loyal to Attlee to contemplate such a challenge and the coup was never attempted. Attlee, perhaps a shrewder leader than they gave him credit for, acknowledged the need for a change in economic policy, appointing Cripps as Minister for Economic Affairs in September 1947.

In November of that year, Stafford Cripps was promoted again when Chancellor Hugh Dalton was forced to resign through a bizarre political miscalculation. On the morning of his 1947 budget statement, Dalton spoke to a reporter from *The Star* newspaper, inadvertently revealing aspects of his financial plan. The journalist was able to get details of the budget into print before the Chancellor made his speech in the House of Commons, thereby breaking a long-established tradition on budget statements. Dalton resigned immediately. Cripps, Minister of Economic Affairs for only two months, now also took over Dalton's post. Cripps was more sympathetic to the use of Keynesian financial levers than Dalton, and on Guy Fawkes Day in 1948, Board of Trade President Harold Wilson announced a 'bonfire of controls', clearly indicating the shift in policy away from direct physical control of the economy and towards a more fiscal approach.

Hugh Dalton, photographed holding up the traditional battered box used on Budget Day, resigned as Chancellor in 1947 following a budget leak after an unwary conversation with a journalist.

Despite its earlier setbacks, the Labour government achieved some notable economic successes. Firstly, it managed to maintain the full employment levels that had been established during the war. Unemployment stood at 2 million in 1938. By 1950, it was down to 400,000, leading Dalton to claim that the attack on unemployment was 'the greatest revolution brought about by the Labour government'. Secondly, it had become clear to the USA that Europe's economic weakness was affecting its own exports. Therefore, under George Marshall a plan was drawn up to assist Europe's recovery from the war, including a substantial loan amounting to $1.2 billion for Britain, which was invested in expanding British exports.

The UK market was economically dependent on the USA in more than one sense. Recession in the USA in 1948 and 1949 triggered a run on the pound, and it became clear to Cripps that a devaluation was necessary. Cripps mishandled the crisis, however, and

The Festival of Britain in 1951 celebrated the optimism of post-war Britain. Its centre was a site on the South Bank of the Thames where exhibitions were housed in a series of imaginative and modern structures. The Festival Hall, designed by Sir Leslie Martin, then Chief Architect for the LCC, is there still (though not the Skylon pointing skywards behind it).

in September 1949 devalued the pound – not to $3 as was widely expected, but to $2.80, which panicked the markets. Further deflationary cuts were then necessary, including a cut in capital expenditure on fuel and power, education and housing.

Yet by the end of the 1940s it could be said that Labour had succeeded in its main economic policy goals. Exports had risen from £266 million in 1944 to £2.2 billion by 1950. Unemployment had remained insignificant throughout Labour's period in office and inflation was low and stable. Difficult decisions had been required, but the government had been able to make them, in sharp contrast to Ramsay MacDonald's Labour government of 1931.

Nato, the Cold War and British withdrawal from Palestine and India

If there was one area of real internal political disagreement, it was over Labour's foreign policy. The Second World War had inspired in some

Labour quarters the desire to seek a 'third way' in foreign policy, which would be equidistant both from Soviet Communism and from US capitalism. Although indicting Britain's imperialist past, these voices still anticipated a leading role for Britain on the world stage. Britain's Foreign Minister, however, had no sympathy with these ideas. The reality of the post-war years, as Ernie Bevin saw it, was that Britain needed to be militarily secure and economically solvent. The Labour government's foreign policy was therefore an attempt to establish strategic agreements to maintain the defence of Britain, while also pursuing a policy of decolonisation in Britain's imperial territories.

Despite the antipathy from Labour's left, the natural ally for Britain was the USA. Immediately after the war ended, Stalin had demonstrated his expansionist ambitions in his negotiations over central Europe, and there were growing Soviet pressures on the Middle East. Bevin's strategy recognised the importance of intertwining the interests of Britain and those of America. Initially the American leadership seemed disinclined to take seriously the threat from Russia or to recognise any responsibility on its part to help. In February 1947, with growing tension in Greece and Turkey, Bevin dropped his bombshell. He informed the US government that Britain was no longer able to take responsibility for the fight against communism in Europe. The American response, in the form of President Truman's speech to Congress in March, was to support Europe financially and to intervene militarily in Europe where necessary. This change in policy, a success for Bevin, brought about the Marshall Plan of US financial help for Europe and led finally to the signing of the North Atlantic Treaty in 1949, which bound the partners together in a pact of mutual defence (NATO).

But of Bevin's achievements were not always appreciated on his own benches in the Commons. In November 1946, a group of Labour MPs moved an amendment to the King's Speech critical of Bevin's strongly anti-Soviet policy, organised around a manifesto entitled *Keep Left* written by Ian Mikardo, Richard Crossman and Michael Foot. Bevin's response, at the 1947 party conference, was to claim that his colleagues had stabbed him in the back. With the Soviet expansion in Eastern Europe in 1947–48, the Keep Left group's equidistant strategy no longer appeared viable. By 1950, the group had split.

The second strand of Bevin's foreign policy was decolonisation. Both Britain's military position and economic circumstances meant that it

A Call for a European Defensive Alliance

We cannot expect that the tension between Russia and America will be reduced in the immediate future, and we shall probably have to plan on the assumption that no agreement between them likely for some time either on the control of atomic energy or on large-scale disarmament. It will be an uneasy and dangerous sort of world.

In these conditions one thing is clear. No European nation will be any safer for taking shelter in either an anti-American or and anti-Russian bloc. The security of each and of all of us depends on preventing the division of Europe into exclusive spheres of influence.

It is here that Britain, working as closely as possible with France, can take the lead. Our immediate aim should be a joint Anglo-French declaration formally abjuring Staff conversations either with the USA or with the USSR. We should make it clear that our joint defence plans will be framed within a regional European security system, according to the terms of the United Nations' Charter and be designed to deter aggression either by Germany or by any non-European Power. Such a declaration would do something to reduce the Russian suspicion that Western Europe is being used for the preparation of war against the Soviet Union.

Keep Left by Richard Crossman, Michael Foot and Ian Mikardo, April 1947

The first weekend for ten years free from petrol rationing was also brilliantly sunny. The roads were packed with cars driving to the sea or the country. This was in May 1950, and austerity was lifting as the British economy started to improve.

was no longer able to maintain colonies across the globe. Furthermore, in particular territories, like India and Palestine, maintaining British rule would have demanded even more resources. Labour's philosophy favoured political freedom for the people of British colonies, and independence movements forced the pace.

In Palestine, the growing Arab-Jewish crisis was reaching a head. The Balfour Declaration in 1917 had promised an independent Jewish homeland in Palestine, with little regard for the rights of the Palestinian Arabs who lived there. Violent anti-semitism in Germany in the 1930s, followed during the war by the systematic elimination of millions of people as the 'final solution' in Nazi policies to 'purify' the German race, resulted in a desperate struggle by the Jewish community across the world to have this promise of a Jewish homeland fulfilled. The USA was sympathetic to their claims, but would offer no support to Britain in managing the Arab-Jewish relationship; neither would the United Nations, although it recommended that Palestine be partitioned. With the situation unresolved, therefore, Britain set a date for withdrawal in 1947, leaving behind an unstable and tragic situation that was quickly to end in war.

Britain also sought rapid withdrawal from India. As in Palestine, there were two forces in India which were heading for conflict, here the Hindu and Muslim communities. Britain's role was viewed with suspicion by both sides and, rather than impose a settlement, Bevin's policy was for Britain to withdraw from the subcontinent in August 1947 leaving two separate nations – India and Pakistan. During partition hundreds of thousands were killed in Hindu-Muslim clashes.

There was one area of foreign policy where Britain sought to maintain its independence from both the USA and the USSR, though not one that was to be approved by the majority of the Keep Left group. In 1946, in a secret cabinet meeting which was not reported until many years later, Attlee gave his agreement to spending £140 million in developing Britain's own atomic capacity. Although the bomb was not tested until

1952, its development gave Britain status as a great power which far exceeded its economic importance in the world.

At the end of 1949, the Labour leadership could look back on their tenure of office with some satisfaction. They had presided over one of the most radical, reforming governments of the twentieth century. Economically, the government had survived an almost impossible financial crisis, and had come out of it with booming exports and full employment. Socially, the Labour government had created a welfare state and health service which were literally the envy of the world. And politically, the government had established a record for not losing a single by-election during its whole five-year term.

Running out of steam: the 1950 and '51 elections

With these achievements already successfully in place, the administration showed marked signs of growing weary of office. The 1949 policy statement had proposed some further nationalisations but there was no attempt to renew the radical spirit of reform that had driven the party to victory in 1945. With so much of its traditional programme fulfilled, it had become more difficult to see the way forward.

The 1950 general election was fought under new electoral circumstances, as the Representation of the People Act of the year before had abolished plural voting for businesses and universities. The election also attracted the highest turnout ever recorded in Britain, at 84 per cent of the electorate. However the results were ambiguous. Labour won 46 per cent and 315 seats, with 1.2 million more votes than in 1945. But the Conservatives won 43.5 per cent of the vote and 298 seats. Labour still had a majority, but it was down to 5. The only clear fact to emerge from the election was that the administration would not be able to last long before going to the country again.

After the election, Attlee reshuffled his team, bringing in Edith Summerskill, doctor and leading feminist, as Minister for National Insurance, moving Dalton to Town and Country Planning and Shinwell to Defence. However, with such a small majority, the pressures on MPs over the next year were intense. This was at a time when many of the older generation were ageing and ill. By October 1950, Cripps was too ill to continue as Chancellor and he was replaced by the young economist and former civil servant, Hugh Gaitskell. Only two years later Cripps had

The general election of 1950 was won by Labour but with only a tiny majority. The campaign posters, reminding voters of all the gains and improvements of the last five years, urged 'Keep it Going', but the Labour old guard was itself running out of energy.

died. Bevin was also troubled by his health, and early in 1951 he stood down, leaving the Foreign Office to Morrison. The declining health of its leading members contributed to the loss of direction in the government. Key figures in the Labour leadership had been in government for over a decade and the party spent its last period in office largely serving out its time. Moreover, Attlee regarded the small majority as a strong indication that Labour no longer had a mandate to implement far-reaching policies. Iron and steel nationalisation went through, but all the other nationalisation plans were dropped.

Nevertheless, the government had to stir itself to cope with an international crisis, which was to precipitate a political crisis at home. June

1950 saw the beginning of the Korean war when North Korea invaded South Korea; the United Nations sent troops, mainly American but also British, against North Korea. The growing international tension led Britain to initiate a programme of rearmament costing over £4.7 billion. The new Chancellor, Hugh Gaitskell, put forward a series of measures in his April 1951 budget to raise the necessary revenue, including raising income tax. But most significant politically was Gaitskell's decision to charge adult patients half the cost of spectacles and dentures.

In fact, the decision to place a charge on some areas of the NHS dated back before the 1950 election. In 1949 there were discussions in cabinet on the spiralling cost of the health service, which only a year after the creation of the NHS had amounted to double the initial estimates. The then Minister of Health, Nye Bevan, believed he had won the first round, by persuading the cabinet to defer any decision until after the election. Following the 1950 election, however, Bevan was appointed Minister for Labour and his successor at the Ministry of Health was removed from the cabinet. Marginalised in the cabinet and facing the imposition of charges on the NHS which he felt was politically unacceptable, Bevan resigned, taking the Board of Trade President, Harold Wilson, and junior minister John Freeman along with him.

In the wake of these decisions and with the party exhausted, Attlee called for a dissolution of parliament in October 1951. The election was a drab affair, focused on whether Churchill could be trusted to maintain peace, and the results were extremely close. In a strange quirk of the electoral system, Labour obtained the most votes, totalling almost 14 million or 48.8 per cent, but 26 fewer seats than the Conservatives. Labour's support was still strong in urban areas but had weakened in the shires. More than six years after the conclusion of the war, Churchill was at last given the chance to lead Britain in peace-time.

The record of the first majority Labour government is rightly regarded as an historic one. It laid the foundations of the post-war world and its achievements were immense and lasting. But by 1951 – or even earlier – the party had run out of steam. Of its leading cabinet members, all except Gaitskell and Wilson had been born in the nineteenth century, before the Labour Party had even been created. It had also been unable to renew itself in office. It was therefore in opposition that Labour would have to continue the debate about the future of the party and the future of socialism.

Chapter Five
The Wilderness Years
1951–1964

Labour's defeat in the 1951 general election ushered in a turbulent period of internal debate and disunity which kept it out of power for thirteen years. It produced an ideological battle about the general aims and values of the party, as well as policy battles over defence and nationalisation. Having created the post-war settlement, Labour was obliged to bequeath it to the Tories and there were those who began to ask whether Labour still had a future. But this period eventually produced the inspired leadership and political skill needed to put Labour back on the road to victory.

Left, right and revisionists

In the aftermath of the 1951 defeat, the vigorous questioning within the party about the nature and future of socialism divided into three main groups. Those on the left wing, known as the Bevanites or 'fundamentalists', had consistently opposed the leadership of the 1945 Labour administration on a range of issues. Led by Nye Bevan, who set down his personal socialist vision in 1952 in his book *In Place of Fear*, the left called for a large programme of nationalisation and for a distinctively socialist foreign policy. On nationalisation, the Bevanites argued that Attlee made too many concessions to public opinion and proposed only a small range of industries for public ownership, while on defence, as we have seen, the left were critical of Bevin's policy of cultivating close relations with the USA.

On the right, Morrison and others saw the Attlee administration not as the first step on the road to socialism but as the achievement of socialism itself. These 'consolidators' were critical of the 'shopping list' approach to nationalisation adopted by the left, and instead restricted their commitments largely to renationalising industries, like iron and steel, that the Conservatives had returned to the private sector. But

In the ideological warfare within the Labour Party in the 1950s, Nye Bevan was the natural focus of the left, particularly after his clash with Gaitskell over NHS charges. Photographed at the 50th party conference in 1951, he stands with other leading left-wingers Harold Wilson (on his right), Ian Mikardo, Tom Driberg and Barbara Castle (on his left).

while the right's shopping list of public ownership was much shorter than the left's, there was little questioning of the role or importance of nationalisation itself.

A third group, however, argued that nationalisation was now irrelevant to socialism. They claimed that socialist policies should instead focus on reducing inequalities in society. These 'revisionists' continued arguments first heard before the war. For example, the economist Evan Durbin had argued in the 1930s that the agenda for democratic socialists was not nationalisation but the harnessing of the virtues of a reformed capitalism to meet the need for security and equality.

It was the experience and lessons of the 1945 Labour government that prompted a revisionist resurgence. A first expression was *New Fabian Essays* (1952) which was intended to mirror the role of the

The intellectual case for Labour 'revisionism' was expressed most cogently by Tony Crosland in *The Future of Socialism*, published in 1956. Opposing the austere vision of old Fabianism, he argued that the key to socialism in post-war Britain was not public ownership but a flourishing economy and social equality.

original 1889 *Fabian Essays in Socialism* in shaping debate about the nature of socialism. Almost without exception, the contributors followed a similar line of argument: that the nature of the British economy and the character of British society had changed, and therefore the character of the socialist alternative must change too. This argument found its fullest expression in the most famous and influential revisionist text of the period, Anthony Crosland's *The Future of Socialism* (1956).

Crosland saw his mission as transforming the Labour Party so that it could meet the challenges of the post-war world. He wanted to be for the British Labour Party what Edward Bernstein had been for the German SPD, and to persuade Labour to embrace the kind of social democratic programme that the German party had recently adopted at Bad Godesberg. But Croslandite revisionism was directed less at old Marxism than at old Fabianism: both its idea of a gradual collectivist road, via nationalisation, to socialism and also the puritanical attitude of the Webbs to liberty, leisure and culture. In providing a theoretical critique of both the left and right, *The Future of Socialism* was to become a generation's revisionist Bible.

Crosland's attack was three-pronged. Firstly, he argued that capitalism had been transformed out of all recognition by successive governments, both before and after the war. There was now a consensus in Britain against laissez-faire economics, no state intervention and poor social provision, while full employment and a welfare state were commitments shared by both parties in government.

Secondly, Crosland insisted that as capitalism had changed, so socialism must change too. He argued that only social welfare and equality were still appropriate concerns for socialists. Public ownership was irrelevant in so far as it did nothing to promote these two aims. Indeed Crosland claimed that those who saw socialism as synonymous with nationalisation were confusing ends and means. Socialism

Changing Solutions for a Changing Society

The need for a restatement of doctrine is hardly suprising. The old doctrines did not spring from a vacuum, or from acts of pure cerebration performed in a monastery cell. Each was the product of a particular kind of society, and of minds reacting to that society. Since this external factor was not constant and unchanging, the doctrines changed through time. And as society has changed again since before the war, so again a restatement of objectives is called for. The matter can be put quite simply. Traditional socialism was largely concerned with the evils of traditional capitalism, and with the need for its overthrow. But to-day traditional capitalism has been reformed and modified almost out of existence, and it is with a quite different form of society that socialists must now concern themselves. Pre-war anti-capitalism will give us very little help.

The Future of Socialism, Anthony Crosland, 1956

consisted of a set of ends, a collection of moral values and beliefs; but the means to these ends were varied and should not be identified simply with nationalisation.

A third point followed from this: new methods of achieving socialism were now needed. Crosland's argument was that the key to socialism was not public ownership but economic growth and social equality. Growth would generate the resources to fund the necessary social welfare provision, while social policy would be an instrument of democratic equality. He also believed that attention would gradually shift from the economic causes of distress to the social and psychological causes – and that there were many inexpensive measures which could improve the quality of life in Britain, including a reform of the laws on homo-sexuality, more open-air cafes, and brighter streets at night. As he put it: 'Total abstinence and a good filing-system are not now the right signposts to the socialist Utopia: or at least, if they are, some of us will fall by the wayside'.

With this intellectual battle taking place in the background, there were also a number of political battles taking place within the Labour Party. The Bevanite group, already united behind a charismatic leader after the resignation of Bevan over the health service charges in 1951, was well-organised and consistently opposed the leadership on a range of issues. The disagreements surfaced in a Commons debate in 1952 on the government's defence estimates. In line with the rearmament pursued by Gaitskell before the election, the Labour leadership supported Churchill's rearmament programme, but recommended abstaining on the vote because of a doubt that the government could carry out the policy. Fifty-seven Labour MPs went further and voted against the estimates for various reasons, which gained them the nickname of the '57 varieties'. Many senior members were incensed by the behaviour of the Bevanites and the episode led to the reinstatement of the Parliamentary Party's Standing Orders, which had been suspended since 1945.

At the 1952 party conference, the Bevanite group continued to act as a thorn in the leadership's side. They succeeded in winning 6 out of 7 of the constituency seats on the National Executive Committee, ousting both Dalton and Morrison. Attlee fought back, condemning what he described as a 'party within the party', and a resolution criticising the organised factionalism of the Bevanites was passed by the Parliamentary Party in October that year by 188 votes to 51.

But Bevan was not easily frustrated. In early 1954 Churchill agreed with the USA that the allies should allow German rearmament. With Attlee and Morrison in favour, the Parliamentary Party was won over to this line, albeit by a small majority, and Bevan resigned from the cabinet in April in order to muster support to reverse the decision at party conference. The result was not to go in his favour. On German rearmament the leadership scraped to victory at conference by 3.3 million votes to 3 million. In fact Bevan suffered a double defeat when he was beaten by Gaitskell for the post of Party Treasurer, vacant after the death of Arthur Greenwood, by a margin of 2 to 1.

Bevan's last main skirmish with the leadership was over the hydrogen bomb. In 1955 the Churchill government had decided to invest in researching a new hydrogen weapon and, while Attlee supported this line, the left argued that a list of restrictions should be placed on the government and abstained from voting on the issue. Worse still, Bevan interrupted Attlee during the winding-up debate and called for clarification of Labour's own policy. The ensuing row within the party resulted

'I Choose Freedom,' proclaimed the headlines when Bevan resigned from Attlee's shadow cabinet in 1954. In the following year this left-wing rebel was almost expelled from the party over his challenge to Attlee during a Commons debate on research into the new hydrogen weapon.

in Bevan having the whip withdrawn and coming close to being expelled from the party altogether, an option which many – including Gaitskell, Dalton and Morrison, but not Attlee – would have preferred.

The victory for the leadership on defence policy in the early 1950s was due in the main to the support of the leading trade unions. Ernest Bevin, the former Foreign Secretary, had been the symbol of close relations between the union movement and the centre-right of the party. But good relations continued after Bevin's death, maintained by the union 'triumvirate' and their leaders: Arthur Deakin at the Transport and General Workers Union, Will Lawther at the National Union of Mineworkers, and Thomas Williamson at the National Union of General and Municipal Workers. However the party was not dominated entirely by the unions in the early 1950s. Individual membership of the party was very large in the post-war period and peaked in 1952 at over one million members, the highest achieved by the party either before or since. But the 'big three' unions controlled a massive block vote, equivalent to about a third of the votes at conference. This was extremely useful for embattled Labour leaders when in a sticky position with the

When Hugh Gaitskell succeeded Attlee in 1955 it was seen as a victory of the revisionist right. A middle-class intellectual rather than a Labour traditionalist, Gaitskell had risen rapidly. He was only forty-nine when he won the leadership over Morrison, who was outraged, and his old antagonist Nye Bevan, whom he then brought into the shadow cabinet.

left-leaning constituency parties. However the close relationship also worked against the party in the run-up to the 1955 election.

Two weeks after the withdrawal of the whip from Nye Bevan, Churchill resigned. He was replaced by his Foreign Secretary, Anthony Eden. The new Prime Minister decided to call a general election at once, aware of the impact that the high number of strikes at the time was having on Labour's popularity. The dockers had gone on unofficial strike in August 1954, followed by a strike of the print workers in March 1955. Then just as this dispute was settled, a national rail strike was threatened for May, the month of the election. These strikes were more damaging to Labour than to the government because of Labour's close relations with the union movement.

The result of the 1955 election was dismaying for Labour supporters: the Conservatives gained almost 50 per cent of the vote, enough to elect 344 MPs and to increase still further their majority in the Commons. Labour's vote remained high, at 12.4 million votes, but the party had certainly lost ground and the new Parliamentary Labour Party was reduced to 277 members.

This second defeat in a row shook the party leadership into action. The first and most immediate result was the withdrawal from senior posts of many of the older generation, including such figures as Dalton, Shinwell and Attlee himself, leaving the field open to a new and younger wave of politicians. The leadership election which followed Attlee's resignation as leader late in 1955 was contested by the old guard in the form of Herbert Morrison. Bevan also stood as the representative of the left. But it was Hugh Gaitskell, having established over the preceding years a large number of sponsors in the trades unions and a growing reputation in the constituencies, who won by a large majority on the first ballot. At forty-nine he was the youngest party leader since Rosebery in 1894. This was all much to Morrison's surprise and dismay and he refused to take the post of deputy leader. Instead this job went to James Griffiths, who had been Minister for National Insurance in Attlee's government, defeating Bevan by 141 votes to 111.

Another consequence of defeat was that the party was forced to examine its own structure. The National Executive Committee appointed a working group, headed by Harold Wilson, to look into the reasons for the defeat and the state of the party's organisation. It reported problems locally, with a shortage of workers and resources, as

Banners proclaimed 'Law not War' as Bevan addressed a mass rally in Trafalgar Square in protest over the British invasion of Egypt in 1956. During the Suez crisis, Labour's strong and concerted attacks on the government reinforced the new moves towards party unity.

well as more serious faults in the national election strategy. 'Compared with our opponents', the report alleged, 'we are still at the penny-farthing stage in a jet-propelled era, and our machine, at that, is getting rusty…with age'. It directed the party to target its efforts on marginal constituencies and modernise its party structures.

A further, if more unexpected, effect of the election defeat was a growth of party unity. Gaitskell was widely regarded as a right-wing leader, but he brought into his shadow cabinet leading members of the left. Wilson became Shadow Chancellor and Bevan Shadow Foreign Secretary. This unity was soon strengthened by the Suez crisis and the fall of Eden. In 1956, as a response to the withdrawal of loans for the Aswan dam project by Britain and the USA, the Egyptian leader Nasser nationalised the Suez Canal Company which managed the canal, a vital route for oil for both Britain and France. Israel attacked Egypt, and on the pretext of keeping Israelis and Egyptians from the canal, Britain and France sent troops to Egypt and occupied Port Said. All this was done without US or United Nations knowledge or support. It is now known and was widely suspected at the time, that France and Britain colluded with Israel over Suez. The crisis also deflected attention from the Russian suppression of the Hungarian uprising of 1956, leading to further criticism of Eden. Under increasing international pressure, including Soviet threats, Eden was forced to order the withdrawal of British forces from the area with nothing achieved, which symbolised to many the humiliating decline of Britain as a world power.

At home, Gaitskell launched an assault on Eden's handling of the crisis. On television the Labour leader denounced Eden as 'utterly discredited in the world' and called for his resignation. His attacks won him recognition and respect across a nation divided between those who saw the Suez venture as dangerous folly and those who were fired with chauvinistic feeling. Gaitskell's criticism intensified the pressure on Eden and in January 1957 he resigned (officially for health reasons) to be replaced by Harold Macmillan.

On the two big political issues of the day, nuclear disarmament and nationalisation, the party followed the lead of Gaitskell. In the debate on defence at the 1957 conference, a motion advocating unilateral nuclear disarmament was defeated by five million votes, with Bevan himself famously attacking the left for threatening to send a future Foreign Secretary 'naked into the conference chamber'. In the same year, the party endorsed *Industry and Society*, which offered a revisionist approach to public ownership. Nationalisation was no longer seen as an end in itself and alternatives to wholesale public ownership were put forward. The document was also passed by a margin of 5 to 1.

Nevertheless, the growth of party unity and 'revisionist' policies were not enough for Labour to win the 1959 general election. Macmillan had managed to restore confidence in the Conservative Party after Suez and, with a 'feel good' period of economic growth, the Conservatives were to run on the slogan, 'Life's better with the Conservatives. Don't let Labour ruin it.' Television was widely used in the campaign for the first time and the Labour Party fought back with some effective television broadcasts. During the run-up to the election, Gaitskell pledged that Labour would not put up taxes, a statement that was construed as a bribe to the electorate. But the result of the election was never really in

'Naked into the Conference Chamber'

If you carry this resolution and follow out all its implications and do not run away from it you will send a British Foreign Secretary, whoever he may be, naked into the conference chamber. Able to preach sermons, of course; he could make good sermons. But action of that sort is not necessarily the way in which you take the menace of this bomb from the world.... What you are saying is what was said by our friend from Hampstead, that a British Foreign Secretary gets up in the United Nations, without consultation – mark this; this is a responsible attitude! – without telling any members of the Commonwealth, without concerting with them, that the British Labour movement decides unilaterally that this country contracts out of all its commitments and obligations entered into with other countries and members of the Commonwealth – without consultation at all. And you call that statesmanship? I call it an emotional spasm.

Aneurin Bevan, Speech at 1957 Labour Party Conference in Brighton

The cartoon labels: LABOUR PARTY / CONSERVATIVE PARTY. Placards read: H-BOMB POLICY, SCHOOLS POLICY, HOUSING POLICY.

doubt. The Conservatives increased their majority yet again, winning 365 seats to Labour's 258. Labour's share of the vote had also dropped sharply, from 46.4 per cent to 43.8 per cent. It was now clear to Gaitskell that, after three successive defeats, Labour needed a more thorough-going review of its aims and values.

Post-mortems, and the battle over Clause IV and unilateral disarmament

The 1959 election defeat precipitated a wide and intense debate about the role, purpose and future of the Labour Party. Outside the party, academics questioned the whole electoral future of the party, in books with such titles as *Must Labour Lose?* Within the party, the economist Douglas Jay wrote an article a few days after the election in which he argued that Labour was too closely associated with the working class. He even suggested that one solution was for the party to change its name; to 'Labour and Radical'. Gaitskell was sympathetic to Jay's thesis (if not to a name change) and at the party conference in November, known as the 'post-mortem conference', proposed an alternative approach of his own. He argued that the party's constitution, specifi-

Television, used for the first time in the 1959 election campaign, was a symbol of the rising prosperity of the 1950s. 'You've never had it so good,' was the theme of Macmillan's campaign, luring voters from Gaitskell and his sheaf of Labour policies.

cally Clause IV (Part IV) which called for the 'common ownership of the means of production, distribution and exchange', should now be updated to reflect changes in the post-war world.

In wanting to revise Clause IV, Gaitskell was challenging what many people at the time regarded as the heart of socialism, equivalent, as Wilson put it, to 'taking Genesis out of the Bible'. Moreover, in recent years the politics of the trade union movement had gradually shifted. For example Deakin, leader of the powerful Transport and General Workers Union, had died in 1956 and had been replaced by the much more left-wing Frank Cousins. It was not surprising, therefore, that Gaitskell faced strong opposition to his plans. Of the old 'big three' unions, only the National Union of General and Municipal Workers backed Gaitskell, while among the party membership there was also much hostility to change. In the face of such opposition, Gaitskell eventually backed down, accepting at the 1960 party conference that no alteration of Clause IV would be made, but instead there would be a new twelve-point plan of the party objectives.

Gaitskell's leadership was weakened by this defeat and it opened the way for a new challenge within the party. Since Bevan's 1957 conference speech, many unilateralists had taken their cause outside the party. The Campaign for Nuclear Disarmament (CND) which emerged out of this group succeeded in recruiting a large number of supporters both inside and outside Labour. After Bevan's death in August 1960 and with Gaitskell on the back foot, the unilateralists chose their moment to reintroduce the nuclear disarmament debate at the 1960 party conference in Scarborough. It was obvious even before the conference that Gaitskell's position was precarious. Several of the unions had changed course under the weight of the CND lobby, and the constituency parties wanted an opportunity to take revenge on Gaitskell for his challenge to Clause IV. At the party conference the unthinkable happened and Gaitskell was defeated. The party passed a motion in favour of unilateral disarmament and rejected the leadership's defence statement.

The defeat on unilateral nuclear disarmament could have meant the end of Gaitskell's leadership, but even before the vote was taken he displayed his intention not to go quietly. Only moments before the ballot, Gaitskell made one of the most dramatic speeches ever delivered by a leader of the Labour Party. He pledged to continue to fight the battle, whatever the result of the conference vote:

Gaitskell listens to Frank Cousins of the TGWU (opposite above) during the 1960 conference debate on unilateral disarmament. After Gaitskell's momentous defeat by the left, he swore to 'fight and fight and fight again'.

The attempt to revise the Labour constitution aroused passionate opposition in the party. 'Hands off Clause Four' placards greeted the members of the NEC, including James Callaghan (opposite below), as they arrived for a special meeting in 1960. Gaitskell backed down.

We may lose the vote today, the result may deal this party a grave blow. There will be many of us who will not accept that the blow must be mortal, who will not believe that such an end is inevitable. There are some of us who will fight and fight and fight again to save the party that we love. We will fight and fight and fight again to bring back sanity and honesty and dignity, so that our party with its great past may retain its glory and its greatness.

Immediately after the defeat, Gaitskell began his campaign to reverse the decision. The battle began with a challenge to his leadership in November 1960 from Harold Wilson. Gaitskell still commanded the majority of the Parliamentary Party and he beat Wilson by the comfortable margin of 166 votes to 81. Part of Gaitskell's strategy was to put more pressure on his colleagues to support him. In one famous incident, Gaitskell chastised a wavering Labour MP: 'You only support me when I'm right. What I need is people who support me when I'm wrong.' He also gained the support of the newly formed Campaign for Democratic Socialism, a centre-right pressure group led by Tony Crosland and Bill Rodgers. By the time of the 1961 Conference in Blackpool, Gaitskell had toured the country and succeeded in winning over the party to his view.

Carrying the distinctive CND symbol and with musicians playing, the Easter 1959 march of the Campaign for Nuclear Disarmament starts off from the nuclear weapons research base at Aldermaston. The concern over a possible nuclear conflict became a matter for increasing public discussion in the 1950s. CND, founded in 1958, rapidly grew into a strong pressure group both nationally and in the Labour Party.

A motion reversing the decision of the 1960 conference was passed by 3 to 1. Gaitskell had fought and won.

The reversal served to rout the left and to restore Gaitskell's position in the party. Moreover, outside it, Gaitskell's courageous stance won him much support. Labour's ratings in the polls had dropped to 37 per cent in October 1960, thirteen points behind the Tories. However by October 1961 Labour had drawn level with the government and a year later the party had opened up a nine-point lead.

Labour's increased popularity was not, of course, all attributable to Gaitskell's leadership. Macmillan's government had run into economic difficulties and was forced to announce an unpopular pay pause to prevent inflation. At this time, Britain also applied for membership of the Common Market. In the 1950s, when discussions about the establishment of a European Coal and Steel Community had begun, Britain had been uninterested in joining. By the early 1960s, however, it was clear that the members of the Community had enjoyed higher rates of economic growth than Britain, and Macmillan began negotiations to join. But on 14 January 1963, the French President Charles de Gaulle used the French veto to block the British application on the grounds that Britain appeared insular, uninterested in the development of Europe and too close to the United States.

Labour's lost leader

With De Gaulle's veto and economic problems besetting the Tories, everything looked set for a Labour victory at the approaching election. Then, less than a week after the veto was announced, the Labour leader was dead. Gaitskell died suddenly, aged only fifty-six, of a complication following a rare illness. Having managed to pull the party back from the brink of destruction to a position where it was the government-in-waiting, Hugh Gaitskell would not be there to lead it into government. Commentators saw the event in terms of a 'lost Prime Minister'. His close friend and ally, Tony Crosland, summed up his own feelings on the announcement of Gaitskell's death: 'My last thought of this man is of his huge vitality, because he was immensely vital, he was as strong as an ox, he was as gay as a child, and it simply seems to me wrong that now he should be dead.'

The leadership election that followed was a battle between Harold Wilson and Gaitskell's supporters who still resented Wilson's challenge

'The White Heat of this Revolution'

In all our plans for the future, we are re-defining and we are re-stating our Socialism in terms of the scientific revolution. But that revolution cannot become a reality unless we are prepared to make far-reaching changes in economic and social attitudes which permeate our whole system of society. The Britain that is going to be forged in the white heat of this revolution will be no place for restrictive practices or for outdated methods on either side of industry... In the Cabinet room and the boardroom alike those charged with the control of our affairs must be ready to think and to speak in the language of our scientific age.

Harold Wilson, speech at the Labour Conference, 1963

Public distaste over the Profumo scandal of 1963 helped to bring down the Macmillan government. Newspaper circulations received a tremendous boost during the summer with the trials that produced revelations in the unravelling of the scandal. Christine Keeler and Mandy Rice Davies, here leaving the Old Bailey, became household names.

in 1960 to their lost leader. However the Gaitskellite vote was now split between George Brown and Jim Callaghan. Brown was the party's deputy leader and had been a strong Gaitskell supporter, but his mercurial talent was flawed with unpredictability and for this reason many could not give him their support. Callaghan had been a protege of Hugh Dalton and was Shadow Chancellor, but he was unlikely to get enough votes to take him through the first ballot. Wilson was therefore the victor. He gained 115 votes on the first ballot to Brown's 88 and Callaghan's 41, and on the second he beat Brown by 144 votes to 103.

Harold Wilson was from a working-class background but he had a classless air. From the Wirral Grammar School, he had won a scholarship to Oxford where he gained a first in Politics, Philosophy and Economics. He had entered parliament in 1945 and within two years his economic expertise and application had put him in the cabinet, at the youthful age of 31. With Bevan he had resigned from the cabinet in 1951, though Wilson later claimed that this was in protest at arms expenditure not health cuts. Whatever the explanation, Wilson's resignation

LET'S *GO* WITH LABOUR FOR THE

NEW BRITAIN

THE LABOUR PARTY'S MANIFESTO FOR THE 1964 GENERAL ELECTION

The Labour election campaign in 1964 (posters above and opposite), struck a chord with a nation that was ready for change. After thirteen years of government, the Conservatives were widely regarded as tired and discredited in the new restless mood of the early 1960s.

won him the reputation of a left-winger, which was both useful and largely undeserved. Wilson was critical of aspects of Gaitskell's leadership, but it was known that he had canvassed for Gaitskell over Bevan in the 1955 leadership contest. And his socialism, detailed by Wilson at the 1963 Labour Party conference, was more about scientific progress and modernisation than nationalisation. His speech on the 'white heat' of Labour's 'scientific revolution' was particularly influential both in the party and in the electorate at large.

After election as leader, Wilson was thrown straight into parliamentary action. In June 1963 John Profumo, the Secretary for War, resigned because he had lied to the House of Commons over his liaison with Christine Keeler who was also linked with a Soviet diplomat. The story and its continuing ramifications became a major scandal, widely reported and satirised in the freer climate that was arriving in the early 1960s. Already unwell, Harold Macmillan chose to resign as Prime Minister in October 1963 and was replaced by the aristocratic and largely unknown Alec Douglas-Home. The general election came a year later and was evenly balanced between the two main parties. Wilson personally spearheaded the Labour campaign and won much support for his style and approach. The party's election manifesto, *The New Britain*, focused on the thirteen wasted years of Conservative government and the planning and social welfare measures that Labour would implement to reverse Britain's relative economic decline. But the battle was so close that even on the morning after the election the result was still unclear. The eventual result was a tiny majority of only 4 for Labour, which had won 317 seats and increased its share of the vote to 44.1 per cent. The Conservatives remained close behind, with 43.4 per cent and 304 seats.

However close, the result marked a watershed in British politics. Labour had been out of power for a generation, rocked by internal strife and arguments about its future, and yet had managed to turn this position around and win office again. And Wilson, defeated in his challenge for the leadership in 1960, found himself four years later – and at the age of only forty-eight – the Prime Minister of a Labour government. After so long a wait, there was a great expectation in the country about the beginning of this second majority Labour administration. The 1960s brought with them a feeling of national change. There was a new mood – and Labour had promised a New Britain.

Let's GO

PUBLISHED BY LABOUR PARTY, TRANSPORT HOUSE, S.W.1 PRINTED BY A.E.A. STUDIOS

with **Labour**

and we'll get things done

Chapter Six
Labour's New Britain
1964–1970

Victory in the 1964 general election marked the beginning of one of the most successful periods in the history of the Labour Party. Although the margin of victory was small, Harold Wilson's government seemed to catch the mood of the 'swinging sixties'. It was out with the old and in with the new, a time of Beatlemania, the contraceptive pill and other new freedoms, when Britain was becoming less stuffy and more modern. The meritocratic figure of Harold Wilson, the grammar school boy from Yorkshire, seemed to personify the new times.

Wilson's style as party leader was in many ways dictated by the size of his parliamentary majority. Unlike Gaitskell before him, Wilson sought to be a moderator and compromiser. His aim was to bring together the different sections of the Labour movement, to unite the Parliamentary Labour Party and so enable the government to survive for as long as possible. Although this approach was eventually to bring its own problems and difficulties, it also brought significant dividends. Not the least of these was that, so long out of office, Labour re-established itself as a party of government.

The first task of the new Prime Minister was to construct his cabinet. In doing so he sought, characteristically, to find a balance between friends and enemies, and between left and right. The key figures in the new government were the two unsuccessful candidates in the 1963 leadership election. James Callaghan became Chancellor of the Exchequer and George Brown became the Secretary of State in charge of Labour's new Department for Economic Affairs. Barbara Castle, the left-wing former member of the Socialist League and old Wilson ally, became the Minister for Overseas Development. Wilson also brought into the cabinet Frank Cousins, the TGWU leader who had caused Gaitskell so many problems. Although he was not an MP, he was given the task of leading the new Ministry for Technology. There were also

Joking with the Beatles in 1964 at an award ceremony, Harold Wilson, not yet fifty, had the right classless style for a Prime Minister in 1960s Britain. The working-class lads from Liverpool, whose music had even conquered the USA, were the irreverent symbol of a new feeling of liberation and boundless opportunity.

The baby dumped on Wilson's doorstep in this Vicky cartoon (published three days after Labour had come into power) has Alec Douglas-Home's face. The Tory leader had left the new government with a huge deficit on overseas payments, partly as a result of Tory attempts to create a boom in the run-up to the election.

posts for old enemies such as Roy Jenkins, Gaitskellite and skilled parliamentary performer, who became Minister of Aviation and with a promise from Wilson of a cabinet post at the first reshuffle (a generous gesture considering Jenkins's relationship with Wilson). Patrick Gordon Walker, also on the right of the party, was appointed Foreign Secretary despite having lost at Smethwick.

The need to make appointments with some speed was linked to Wilson's election promise that his government would launch a bold 'first hundred days' of reform. But he did not rely solely on his cabinet for direction and drive. Also appointed were a number of advisers and specialists, known in some circles as the 'kitchen cabinet', brought in to assist the Wilson government on economic, political and security matters. Such a move was to be repeated by later Prime Ministers without much controversy, but at the time the activities and influence of a shadowy body of advisers was a source of some discontent and suspicion within both the Labour Party and the civil service. This kitchen cabinet served to strengthen Wilson's already dominant position in the Parliamentary Party and the cabinet.

Another reason for speedy action was the economic situation the Labour government had inherited from the Conservatives. While the election campaign had been fought on Wilson's claim that the Tories had created an economic mess, it was not until after the election victory that the state of the books revealed its true extent. Labour inherited a massive (for the time) £800 million deficit on overseas payments, and even before the election dust had settled the new government faced a crisis of confidence in sterling. As Wilson noted in his personal record of the government: 'It was this inheritance which was to dominate almost every action of the government for five years of the five years, eight months we were in office'.

Faced with this crisis, within twenty-four hours of the election victory and before Wilson, Brown and Callaghan had even had a chance to catch up on lost sleep, the three men took the key decision not to devalue the pound. Devaluation was the option suggested by most of the leading Labour economists. Immediately after the election, the economic crisis and a forced devaluation could legitimately have been pinned on the former Conservative government. Without devaluation, many recognised how difficult it would be for a Labour government to encourage exports and foster the higher economic growth that it needed for its social programme.

Despite all these considerations, Harold Wilson was steeled against devaluation. He had been involved in the Attlee government's devaluation of the pound and did not want Labour to gain a reputation as the party of devaluation. Devaluation would symbolise Britain's declining world role politically. It would also mean going back on an election promise within days of forming a government. While it has become easy with hindsight to criticise Wilson's position, it was not clear to many leading politicians at the time that devaluation would be beneficial to the economy. In the event the government was forced to defend its position with ever-increasing vigour, making it more difficult each time for the government to rethink its policy and change direction on this key economic issue.

With devaluation ruled out, the government immediately imposed a 15 per cent import surcharge in a desperate effort to stabilise the pound. But any respite was short-lived. The new Chancellor Callaghan's first budget, while ambitiously attempting to keep to Labour's promises for the abolition of prescription charges and increases in pensions, precipitated a further weakening of sterling on a nervous market. The bank rate was raised to 7 per cent and loans of $3,000 million were raised by international banks. The pound recovered and the new government's immediate economic crisis was over. It was a first taste of what was to come.

The Devaluation Dilemma

There was comment, and this has been subsequently echoed, that we made an initial, even a fatal, blunder in our decision not to devalue within twenty-four hours of taking office, when we could have put all the responsibility on our Conservative predecessors. Politically, it might have been tempting and we were not unaware of the temptation. But I was convinced, and my colleagues agreed, that to devalue could have the most dangerous consequences.

The financial world at home and abroad was aware that the post-war decision to devalue in 1949 had been taken by a Labour government. There would have been many who would conclude that a Labour government facing difficulties always took the easy way out by devaluing the pound. Speculation would be aroused every time that Britain ran into even minor economic difficulties – or even without them. For we were to learn over the years that it was all too easy for those so minded to talk the pound down on the most frivolous of pretexts.

Harold Wilson, *The Labour Government 1964-70,* 1971

The first hundred days of reform

Despite this baptism of fire, the new administration laid down its plans for reform in its first Queen's Speech in November. As well as the social measures contained in Callaghan's budget, the speech also contained plans for steel nationalisation, rent controls, a land commission, union legislation and a free vote on the death penalty. Wilson added fury to the Queen's Speech debate when he called on the Conservative leader to disassociate himself from Peter Griffiths, the new Tory MP for Smethwick, who had been accused of running a racist campaign in defeating Patrick Gordon Walker. Inflaming the Conservative benches, Wilson declared that the new member for Smethwick 'will serve his time there as a parliamentary leper'.

Even with its tiny majority, Harold Wilson's government went a long way towards implementing the legislation it had pledged in its manifesto. The 1965 Rent Act reversed the 1957 Act, known as the 'landlords' charter', by fixing fair rents for private tenants and providing security of tenure. The Redundancy Payments Act provided for payments for workers who lost their jobs through no fault of their own, while the Race Relations Act outlawed racial discrimination and established a

Britain's post-war shortage of labour had been partly met by the immigration of Afro-Caribbean and Asian citizens of the Commonwealth. Labour's Race Relations Act and Race Relations Board of 1965 were a recognition that discrimination and racism, which had erupted into violence in the 1958 Notting Hill riots, were unacceptable in a free and democratic society.

Even the dog seems spellbound by George Brown's flamboyant oratory. Brown, a brilliant if erratic politician and a Gaitskellite, first discussed setting up the new Department for Economic Affairs in a taxi ride with Wilson. The DEA, intended to revitalise the British economy under a National Plan, suffered from Brown's unreliability and was constantly marginalised by the Treasury.

Race Relations Board. The government also encouraged local authorities to develop plans for the extension of comprehensive education. In allowing a free Commons vote on the death penalty, the result brought about the suspension of capital punishment until 1970. The only real disappointment was over steel nationalisation. Faced with strong Tory opposition and some dissent from the right wing of the party, the government only just managed to scrape a victory on the White Paper proposing the nationalisation of the leading steel companies. The margin was such that there was little chance to pass legislation before a general election, and the plans were shelved.

The refusal to devalue sterling was soon to have a serious effect on the Labour government's strategic attempts to achieve improved economic growth. A Department for Economic Affairs (the DEA) had been set up under George Brown with the purpose of introducing planning into the British economy. The first National Plan was duly unveiled on 16 September 1965, including targets for public expenditure and growth, and plans for improving exports. The DEA was unable to make a real impact, however, and before the decade was out the new Department was scrapped.

Part of the problem was a matter of personality. George Brown combined talent with unreliability and his legendary drinking habits lost him the confidence of many colleagues. Some of Wilson's critics were prepared to overlook his misdemeanours ('better George drunk than Harold sober', as one put it) but Brown was unable to win for the Department any real authority within Whitehall and the new DEA was easily side-stepped by Treasury officials.

There was a more profound problem with Labour's growth strategy. Because of Wilson's adamant refusal to devalue the pound, the National Plan was gradually sacrificed in order to protect the rate of sterling. Not only was export growth difficult because of the exchange rate, but the government was forced into deflationary measures to stabilise the currency. Labour economists inside and outside the cabinet were increasingly critical of the strategy, but Wilson vetoed any discussion of the issue. Within cabinet circles, devaluation became known as 'the unmentionable'.

Politically the position of the Labour government was precarious from the outset, but it was made even more unstable in January 1965 with the loss of the Leyton by-election. The seat was fought in order to enable the Foreign Secretary Patrick Gordon Walker to re-enter the Commons. However this 'safe' Labour seat was lost by a 8.7 per cent swing to the Conservatives. Gordon Walker was obliged to resign as Foreign Secretary, to be replaced by Michael Stewart, leaving a vacancy for Tony Crosland to enter the Cabinet as Secretary of State for Education. On the same day as the Leyton election, Frank Cousins also managed only to scrape to victory in a by-election at Nuneaton arranged for a similar purpose. A tiny majority had become even tinier.

With Labour's position slipping during the summer of 1965, Wilson attempted to restore political and economic confidence by ruling out another general election that year. This statement precipitated further political turmoil, but this time in the ranks of the Conservatives. Alec Douglas-Home, the Conservative leader, had managed to survive a challenge after the 1964 election defeat because there was a strong chance of another election in the near future. When Wilson ruled this out, the 'men in grey suits' went in their time-honoured Conservative fashion to see their leader, and his resignation was duly tendered in July 1965. Douglas-Home's replacement was the modernising meritocrat Edward Heath, who beat Reginald Maudling in the first election ever held for the Tory leadership.

The Conservative pre-occupation with the leadership election handed the initiative back to Wilson. But he was dogged over the summer by the growing US involvement in the war between North and South Vietnam, which caught him in a pincer between his American creditors and his left-wing back-

It was an accusation of the 1960s, bluntly put, that America supported the pound, and Britain supported America in Vietnam. Scarfe's famously savage humour at the expense of Britain's often-invoked special relationship with the USA was a reflection of profound and growing opposition to US involvement in Vietnam.

I'VE HEARD OF A SPECIAL RELATIONSHIP, BUT THIS IS RIDICULOUS

VIETNAM

WILSON RIGHT BEHIND JOHNSON

Gerald Scarfe

In 1965 Harold Wilson tried to talk Ian Smith out of a unilateral declaration of independence for Southern Rhodesia, Britain's last colony in Africa, but without success. After three years of sanctions, the two met again on board *HMS Fearless* in Gibraltar (above), but came to no agreement. The rebellion lasted not weeks, as Wilson had predicted, but thirteen years.

benchers. In June 1965 Wilson attempted to bring together Commonwealth leaders to lead a peace mission to Vietnam, but it was more of a tactical move than real statesmanship, and the proposal came to nothing. Meanwhile another foreign policy problem needed even more urgent attention. In 1964 Southern Rhodesia's request for full independence had been refused because its black majority was ruled by a white minority. In May 1965, Ian Smith and his Rhodesia Front won a landslide victory in the country's elections and immediately pushed for independence from Britain. Wilson sought to negotiate with Smith, a skilled and shrewd politician, and in October even visited Rhodesia. However these talks were unproductive, and in November 1965 Rhodesia declared unilateral independence. Wilson responded by imposing oil sanctions on the country and confidently predicted Smith's downfall within 'weeks not months'. Events were to prove otherwise.

Despite growing worries in the party that Wilson may have waited too long to call the inevitable general election, his strategy was vindicated by a by-election in Hull in January 1966. Predictions that the party would lose the seat proved unfounded as Labour comfortably retained

Hull North with a 4.5 per cent swing to the government. Boosted by this result, Wilson set the date for the general election – 31 March – and began working on the party's manifesto, *Time for Decision*. Labour's campaign, with its slogan 'You know Labour Government works', was now focused largely on the strength of Wilson's leadership and on the need for a clear mandate to complete its programme.

March 1966: Wilson is given a new mandate in the general election

The result of the election was widely predicted in the media and opinion polls. Labour increased its share of the vote to 48 per cent, winning 363 seats and giving it a majority of almost 100 over the other parties. The Liberals, with 8.5 per cent, had managed to increase the number of their MPs to 12. Wilson had been given the mandate to finish the job. Not only that, but for the first time ever, an outgoing Labour government had increased its majority.

The implications of the election victory were not all good for Wilson. While he had won a much bigger majority in the House of Commons, the new security of the government's position also served to encourage political dissent on the Labour benches. Practising his golf swing with the Prime Minister at Chequers just after the 1966 election, a visiting foreign President asked Wilson, 'How's your handicap, Harold?' 'Up from 3 to 97', came Wilson's retort.

The Queen's Speech of 1966 largely consisted of what Labour had promised in its party manifesto: steel nationalisation; the development of comprehensive education; the establishment of an Industrial Reorganisation Corporation; and renegotiation for membership of the European Economic Community. But any idea of a post-election honeymoon period was shattered by the seamen's strike in May 1966 which blew Wilson's government off course.

The seamen's strike had its origins in a normal battle over pay, but it became a hot political issue because of the government's growing need to control prices and incomes. In the face of mounting criticism from the trade union movement, the government backed the employers and criticised the seamen's pay demands. Wilson made an already sensitive political issue even more acute by claiming that the strikers were 'a tight knit group of politically motivated men', implying widespread communist infiltration. The strike was also damaging economically, with

The seamen's strike of May 1966 brought Wilson's government into conflict with the unions only two months after its new mandate from the electorate. Struggling to control prices and incomes, it was not sympathetic to the seamen's demands, and Wilson's dark hints of communist influence among the strikers widened the rift.

the financial markets uncertain whether the government would be able to continue its economic strategy without the support of the unions.

The government's response was to tighten the control over prices and incomes. The Prices and Incomes Board, which had been set up in 1965, was strengthened by a Bill in July 1966 which forced companies and unions to give advance warning of any wage or price increases. The Board then had the power to postpone any increase until it had been considered. This policy was attacked by the left and led to the resignation of Frank Cousins, the former Secretary of the Transport and General Workers Union and Minister for Technology.

But the policy did not satisfy the markets either, and on 20 July the government was forced into a package of deflationary measures to stabilise the currency, including a legally binding six-month freeze on prices and wages. The proposals not only marked the realistic end of the National Plan, but they also triggered a mini-revolt within the cabinet by the pro-devaluation group. This was only abated by Wilson's pledge to set up a cabinet committee to discuss economic strategy. Yet even on this committee, called the Steering Committee for Economic Policy, the 'unmentionable' was still off the agenda. Another political outcome of the economic crisis of the summer was the further decline of George Brown. Having threatened to resign on several occasions, he was shifted in August 1966 to the post of Foreign Secretary, swapping with Michael Stewart who went to the DEA, and stayed in that post until he did finally resign in the spring in 1968.

Devaluation, the 'unmentionable' : 'the pound in your pocket…'

The painful economic measures taken by the Wilson government appeared for a time to have worked. By the end of 1966 the balance of payments was running at a surplus and in early 1967 record export figures were achieved. However in the second half of that year the pound once again came under pressure after the announcement of falling gold reserves. Together with uncertainty caused by Britain's application to join the Common Market, rising unemployment and dock strikes in Liverpool and London, the situation was becoming unsustainable and something had to give. In November it did. On 18 November Wilson announced the reversal of his key economic strategy. Sterling was to be devalued from $2.80 to $2.40. In a television broadcast, the Prime Minister tried to portray the decision in its best possible light. Devaluation, he argued, freed Britain from the straitjacket of the past and allowed for export opportunities and the hope of renewed growth. But Wilson's famous comment that devaluation did not mean 'that the pound here in Britain, in your pocket or purse or in your bank has been devalued' was seized upon for attack by the government's opponents.

Chancellor Jim Callaghan was broken by the devaluation and he felt honour bound to stand down, but to keep him in the cabinet Wilson swapped him with Roy Jenkins at the Home Office. The devaluation was also followed by the need for a loan from the International Monetary Fund (IMF), which came with conditions attached of further deflationary measures. Jenkins's first year as Chancellor was therefore dominated by the severe measures that would restore Britain's economic position. But by the summer of 1969 the balance of payments was in surplus and predictions of a devaluation-led export boom seemed to have been proved right. In December the renewed economic confidence led to the pound topping its parity level of $2.40.

Despite being plagued for much of its life by these economic difficulties, the government nevertheless managed notable successes in the field of social reform. The sphere of comprehensive education was expanded, and the pioneering Open University was created to offer access to higher education from the home. The 1969 Representation of the People Act extended the vote to eighteen-year-olds, and in December of the same year the abolition of capital punishment was made permanent. Barbara Castle spearheaded the legislation to provide equal pay for women in the workplace in 1970. The government also offered support to three Private Members' Bills which were to transform the nature of British society. The 1967 Sexual Offenders Act made homosexual acts legal between consenting adults over twenty-one. The Medical Termination of Pregnancy Act introduced provisions for abortions through the health service, and the Divorce Reform Act made divorce possible on grounds of the irretrievable breakdown of marriage. It was a period of social revolution in which Wilson's Labour administration played a major part.

The government also attempted to make radical reforms to the way parliament ran Britain. In 1964, the first Queen's Speech had announced the government's intention to create a Parliamentary Commissioner or Ombudsman, to enable the public to voice grievances about the actions

The Open University was a Labour achievement that Harold Wilson was particularly proud of. It gave students the opportunity to study for a degree at home through special radio and television broadcasts. Students' contact with their tutors was through correspondence and summer schools (below).

In 1968 the scenes outside the US Embassy in London's Grosvenor Square reflected the strength of anti-American feeling over Vietnam, reinforced by pictures of the horrors of war appearing in the media. 1968 was a year of student political protest in Britain and reflected the widespread political turbulence at the time, notably in Paris and Prague.

of parliament and MPs. This was backed up in 1967 by the creation of Select Committees in the Commons. Established by the Leader of the House, Richard Crossman, who had been a contemporary of Gaitskell at Winchester and leader of the Labour group on Oxford City Council, the Committees enabled MPs to examine policy in greater detail and even criticise the actions of the executive. Wilson also planned far-reaching reform of the House of Lords, scrapping the powers of hereditary peers, restricting the Lords' delaying powers to six months, and making sure that governments had a working majority in the Lords' Chamber. However an unlikely alliance of Labour's left and the Conservative right, personified by Michael Foot and Enoch Powell, opposed the legislation. Foot was concerned that the changes would give the Lords too much power, Powell that the reforms would take too many powers away, but the alliance united to 'talk out' the Bill and the planned reforms were lost.

Race relations were also difficult for the Labour government to handle. Labour had demonstrated its commitment to the issue in 1965 when it passed the first Race Relations Act and this commitment was reinforced by a further Act in 1968. At the same time, the government introduced an Immigration Bill restricting the use of British passports,

In 1967 Britain made its second application to join the Common Market. Although Wilson's baggage – commitments to the Commonwealth, the shaky economy, East of Suez foreign policy – all gave De Gaulle reasons to bar entry, he was chiefly afraid of losing France's dominating position in the EEC. After his resignation in April 1969, British negotiations were renewed.

in response to growing fears about the numbers of Kenyan Asians fleeing from their government's hardline Africanisation policies. It was a difficult course to steer at a time when Enoch Powell's 'Rivers of Blood' speech in Birmingham in 1968 had heightened the general tension over race and immigration in Britain .

Other issues also pressed in. The government's bid to enter Europe had been met yet again by De Gaulle's veto. But the French President's resignation in April 1969 enabled the government to negotiate once again for entry and by the end of the parliament Labour had put Britain's application back on track. The union of the United Kingdom also started to crack at the edges. Sectarian violence in Northern Ireland led to the intervention by the British army in 1969 in an attempt to restore peace, the beginning of a generation of unresolved conflict in that troubled province. In Wales and Scotland there were growing demands for greater political independence, symbolised by victories in by-elections for the Scottish National Party and Plaid Cymru, also harbingers of the policies of devolution that were to come.

Strife over 'In Place of Strife'

With mounting criticism of his leadership, Wilson faced another setback. This time it was in the form of industrial relations. Already conscious of the need to keep a tight hold on wages, the government put forward proposals in January 1969 for the reform of trade unions to curb unofficial strikes. The plans were detailed in a paper called *In Place of Strife*, written by the Secretary of State for Employment Barbara Castle. It was widely opposed both inside the Parliamentary Party and outside it, largely because it involved legal sanctions forcing unions to ballot members on strike action and imposed a twenty-eight-day cooling off period before strike action could begin. James Callaghan led the critics from within the cabinet and there was opposition from many others who were concerned at the political as well as the industrial impact of the proposals. By June 1969 it had become clear that the level of opposition to the plans was such that if the Prime Minister went

Barbara Castle had moved from Transport to Employment in 1968. Her diaries record her frustration at the time spent on industrial disputes, while trying to control wages. But *In Place of Strife,* her proposals for union reform, caused such opposition that she and Wilson found themselves isolated. Her career never really recovered, and the row damaged the party.

ahead, the Bill would be defeated. Barbara Castle, backed down and settled instead for a voluntary agreement by which unions would obey the TUC guidelines. But by then the political damage – and it was considerable – had already been done.

It was no surprise that the Labour government had trailed the Conservatives in the opinion polls from 1967 onwards. A month after the devaluation, Labour was 17 points behind, with its share of voters' support down to 32 per cent. But improving economic circumstances turned this situation around, and by October 1969 the Conservative

The Shock of the 1970 General Election Result

Polling Day. Caroline and I went round the polling stations. It is part of a ritual but it has to be done and it is very tiring…After we had completed the polling stations and committee rooms and loudspeaker work, we were pretty sure of victory by twenty or thirty…

At 11.15 we got the first result and it showed an enormous swing to the Tories and, all of a sudden, there and then, we realised we had lost the election…

Harold was not conceding the result but biding his time and I spared a thought for the poor man believing himself due to continue as Prime Minister and discovering he had been defeated.

Tony Benn, *Office Without Power: Diaries 1968–1972*,
Thursday 18 June 1970 (General Election day)

lead over Labour was reduced to 2 per cent. In 1970, with economic recovery continuing, Labour did well in the local elections and on the back of these successes Wilson called a general election for 18 June.

Opinion polls the weekend before the election consistently predicted a Labour victory. In fact, many betting shops had stopped taking money on Labour winning. The election result was therefore a severe blow to Harold Wilson and the Labour Party. Believing that their political fortunes had recovered enough to win, the result brought a narrow Conservative victory. Labour saw its share of the vote drop from 48 per cent in 1966 to 43 per cent, leaving it with only 287 seats. More worrying still in the long term, the 1970 election also marked the beginning of the fragmentation of Labour's traditional working-class vote. While support for Labour remained steady in other social classes, among working-class voters it declined from 70 per cent in 1964 to 60 per cent in 1970. The seeds of future electoral problems were already in place, although this was not clear at the time.

Despite the election defeat, Wilson was able to stay on as party leader. He had won Labour two elections and it was possible he would win more for the party. His period as Prime Minister was constantly beset by economic and industrial difficulties, but it is a tribute to his style of leadership that his government was able to achieve the successes it did. Wilson was dominant in government, effective with the public and had a pragmatic populism which enabled him to draw support from all sections of the party. As his biographer, Ben Pimlott, describes it, Wilson often 'seemed like a juggler spinning plates on sticks, moving rapidly from one to the next to keep all in motion, while maintaining a witty patter to the audience at the same time.'

After the devaluation, nevertheless, the Labour leader's juggling act started to come undone and some of the plates began to fall off. It had been Wilson's decision to defend sterling at all costs and it increasingly became a compromise that neither left nor right wanted. The confrontation over *In Place of Strife* caused much damage and undermined the government's credibility. Yet the legislative record of the Wilson administration was impressive. It had undoubtedly been a period of social reform and modernisation on many fronts, with an enduring legacy. And in party terms, Labour had thrown off its long years in opposition and done much to establish Harold Wilson's claim for it as the party of government.

Chapter Seven
In and Out of Power
1970–1979

Histories of the 1970s have not usually portrayed the Labour Party or its leading figures in a favourable light. Despite an improving economic situation, the decade began with the party losing the general election and facing the prospect of another lengthy period in opposition. With the party out of office, growing divisions also appeared between the left and right over issues such as nationalisation and entry into Europe. A deteriorating economic and social climate meant that, even when the party was narrowly returned to power in 1974, it not only struggled to deliver the 'fundamental shift in power and wealth' that its manifesto spoke of but also found itself rocked by the inflationary and industrial turbulence of a decade that seemed to mark the end of the post-war world and its underlying assumptions. A traditional politics was being subverted. Yet, while the party may have attained less than it had hoped, there were some real achievements in this period. Not the least of these was Labour's ability to win elections. Right up until the 1979 election, many thought that Labour had become the natural party of government and that the Conservatives were in serious decline. It may have been an illusion; but for much of the 1970s it was a plausible view.

Labour in opposition: the great divide on Europe polarises the party

The result of the 1970 general election was a shock for Labour, and especially for Harold Wilson. Instead of leading the country and the party into another term, Wilson returned to the opposition benches. But he was determined to hang on to the party leadership, and at fifty-four he was still young in terms of a political career. With his characteristically skilful manoeuvring he managed to avoid an immediate leadership challenge and, in order to retain party unity, he backed his main opponent, Roy Jenkins, in the contest for deputy leader.

The Heath government that came to power in 1970 had to face a series of crises. One of the most serious was in 1973 when Arab countries restricted the supply of oil following the Israeli–Egyptian war of that year, and oil prices soared. The shortage of petrol caused long queues of cars.

It is not unusual for political parties to develop factious and divisive tendencies in opposition, when the pressures of office recede and new directions can be explored, but in the 1970s, Labour's divisions were especially acute. On a range of issues, but with Europe never far from the foreground, the party became increasingly polarised between left and right. Wilson's job, as ever, was to try to bind the two groups together. It was a task for which he was well-equipped, but even his abilities were increasingly tested to the limits.

The new Prime Minister, Edward Heath, continued the strategy which Labour had begun for taking Britain into the Common Market – the European Economic Community. There was mounting dissent in the Labour Party over these proposals, which came to a head in January 1971 when 119 Labour MPs signed a Commons early-day-motion against the terms of entry to Europe that Heath had secured. The ex-Chancellor Jim Callaghan championed the anti-EEC cause and managed to rally substantial support from other MPs and the constituency parties. At the same time the pro-Europe lobby was also organising strongly, with Roy Jenkins and the former Minister for Education and Science, Shirley Williams, as key figures.

Wilson worked feverishly to find a position which would satisfy everyone, ever conscious of the growing anti-European feeling in the party. In 1971 Labour held a summer conference on Europe, which was a useful sounding-board but did not have any binding vote, and then in July the NEC voted against entering Europe on the existing terms by 16 votes to 6. The Parliamentary Party and conference also followed this line later in the year. Whatever its merits, the party's stance certainly involved some political gymnastics on Wilson's part. He denied that the terms obtained by Heath were the same as those he would have accepted had he been returned to office in 1970. Yet he also denied that the party was fundamentally opposed to Europe. His line was that it was simply a question of renegotiating the terms of entry.

Heath allowed a free vote on the government's terms of entry, conscious that there was a substantial group of Labour pro-marketeers prepared to enter the government lobby. Labour MPs were instructed by their whips to vote against the terms, but 69 'Euro-rebels' defied the whips and a further 20 abstained. Notwithstanding the votes of several anti-European Conservatives, the government's terms of entry were endorsed with a substantial majority.

The question of entry into Europe continued to divide the party, and Wilson in opposition was steering a difficult path between those for and those against. This 1971 cartoon by Mahood sums up part of the dilemma. The Ford workers, a byword for union militancy in the Tory press, relish the thought of striking for the higher wages earned in the EEC.

"It's a great opportunity brothers, we could go on strike for parity with Volkswagen, Fiat, Renault . . ."

Yet the passing of the legislation on Europe only served to create more problems for Labour. Having been taken into Europe, the question now was whether Labour would take Britain out again. In search of an answer, Wilson took up the suggestion of Anthony Wedgwood Benn for a national referendum on British entry into Europe. Wedgwood Benn, heir to Lord Stansgate, had campaigned brilliantly for the right to renounce hereditary peerages, and disclaimed his in 1963 so that he could keep his seat as MP for Bristol East. He had been a pro-Marketeer as Wilson's enthusiastic Minister for Technology from 1966 to 1970. His notion of a referendum, far from uniting the party, was the defining moment which formalised the split within its ranks. The proposal was the final straw for Roy Jenkins, who resigned as deputy leader. Other pro-Europeans left too, including George Thomson and Harold Lever. More significantly, the party's stance on Europe clearly indicated the increasing dominance of the left. Left-wingers had taken a growing number of positions on the National Executive Committee and within the Parliamentary Party. Many on the right of the party, who were now largely regarded as 'rebels', were either on the backbenches or out of the Commons altogether. This growing divide was a sure recipe for eventual electoral disaster.

U-turns and the three-day week under Heath's government

In the short-term, though, it was the Tories not Labour who were plumbing the depths of electoral unpopularity. Heath had been elected on a platform of economic reform. Formal incomes policies were to be scrapped, as was the Industrial Development Corporation. The government discontinued Labour's policy under Benn of helping industries in trouble – 'lame ducks' – and made cuts to public expenditure by abolishing free milk for school children and increasing prescription charges. But the real problem for the Heath government was the emergence of 'stagflation', a combination of high inflation and the stagnation signalled by rising unemployment. Inflation averaged 8.6 per cent between 1970 and 1973, while unemployment – which had peaked at 595,000 in 1969 – rose to almost one million in 1972. At the same time, the Conservative approach to industrial relations resulted in more strikes than under Labour: 6.8 million working days were lost through strikes in 1969, but by 1972 this had rocketed to 24 million days.

Riots in Belfast's Andersonstown (above) in protest at the presence of British soldiers. The troubles in Northern Ireland escalated into crisis in 1972, and direct rule from Westminster was imposed. British troops had first gone to Ulster in 1969 after street battles between Catholics and Loyalists. In 1972 thirteen demonstrators were shot dead by British troops in Derry.

The uncomfortable economic circumstances led to a famous series of 'U-turns'. The 'no lame ducks' policy was abandoned as the government intervened in industries in difficulty, notably Rolls Royce and ship-builders on the Upper Clyde. Then a formal prices and incomes policy was introduced, supported in November 1972 with the creation of a Price Commission, and the Industrial Development Corporation, scrapped by the government in 1970, was replaced in 1972 by an Industrial Development Executive.

Already besieged with economic problems, the Heath administration was further hit by the development of two conflicts. Firstly, the already explosive situation in Northern Ireland erupted in clashes between nationalists and the army. On 30 January 1972, as a march for civil rights for Catholics broke out into a riot, thirteen people were shot dead by the armed forces in Londonderry's Bogside; it was a day that became known as 'Bloody Sunday'. In March 1972, facing a mounting crisis and criticism from all sides, the government suspended the powers of the Northern Ireland Parliament at Stormont and introduced direct rule from Westminster. There was also much criticism, from nationalists and many Labour members, of the government's introduction (under new emergency powers) of internment without trial of suspected members of the Irish Republican Army.

While the situation in Northern Ireland was to trouble British politicians for decades to come, a second crisis had a more immediate impact on Britain's economy. In October 1973, just as the Heath government was to begin the next stage of its counter-inflationary policy, the Yom Kippur conflict broke out between Egypt and Israel. Arab countries restricted the sale of oil, on which Britain depended, and the price of oil on the international market rose dramatically. This also had a disastrous effect on Britain's already high balance of payments deficit. Heath had inherited a surplus of almost £500 million from Wilson, but by 1973, the balance of payments was a billion pounds in the red.

The final straw for the Conservative government was an industrial dispute by the miners in 1973. In November 1973 the National Union of Mineworkers (NUM) began an overtime ban to support a pay claim which exceeded the limits of the government's incomes policy. Heath had been forced to give way to the miners' demands once before in 1972, and this time he decided to hold firm, but the miners gained the support of power engineers, and on 13 November the government declared a state of emergency, with restrictions on the use of electricity. This was followed by the introduction of a three-day week for industry on 1 January 1974, restrictions of 50 m.p.h. on all roads, with television channels and offices forced to close at 10.30 pm.

The hope of a settlement disappeared when talks broke down and on 10 February the miners voted for an all-out strike. Overwhelmed by economic crises, Heath used the strike as a reason for calling a general election on the theme of 'Who runs Britain?' He attempted to portray Labour as the party of unruly union militancy, and the Conservatives as tough enough to fight vested interests. Wilson's response was to present Labour as the party of conciliation and sensible industrial relations, contrasting this with the Tories' incompetence and instability. Labour's strategy was also to remind the voters that the party had got Britain out of the economic mess left by the Tories in the 1960s and stood ready to do the same again in the 1970s.

Miners and Housewives in Heath's Firing Line

I welcome this Election – I welcome, more than anything else, this opportunity for the British people to give their verdict upon the last three years and eight months of Conservative Government. Let the people vote; let us work together again…

The Government called this election in panic. They are unable to govern and dare not tell the people the truth…

The British people were never consulted about the Market. Even more, the country was deceived in 1970 about the Government's intention on jobs and prices. They will not be deceived again. Today the people of Britain know that reasonable leadership by Government can achieve an honourable settlement of the mining dispute and get the country back to work. Only stubborn refusal by an arrogant Conservative administration stands in our way.

The new Labour Government will see that the present dispute is settled by negotiation. We shall control prices and attack speculation and set a climate fair enough to work together with the unions.

This Election is not about the miners. They are in the firing line today. The housewife has been in the firing line ever since Mr Heath was elected. Let us now choose a Government willing to face up to Britain's problems; let us elect a Government of all the people; let us work together.

Foreword by Harold Wilson to the 1974 Labour Manifesto –
Let us Work Together – Labour's Way out of the Crisis

Harold Wilson appears on screen in Trafalgar Square as the 1974 election results come in. The Labour win came as a surprise to most people, not least Wilson himself. Wilson made it clear that, although he would be heading a minority Labour government, he would carry on as if he had a Commons majority.

Labour's election campaign had some unlikely supporters, notably Enoch Powell, the arch-Tory right-winger, infamous for his 1968 inflammatory 'rivers of blood' speech on immigration. Strongly anti-European, he stood down from re-election to parliament as a result of Heath's pro-European policies. But more damaging still, he advised Conservative voters to back the Labour Party because of its commit-ment to a referendum on the Common Market. Powell even organised for himself a postal vote so that, with only a few days to go before the election, he could prove that he had already voted Labour.

Labour wins the 1974 election, but with a majority of only four

For all his failings as Prime Minister, there was a wide expectation that Heath would win a second term in office. By contrast, Wilson expected defeat and was widely reported to be already planning his retirement. As in 1970, the result of the election came as a surprise to pundits and

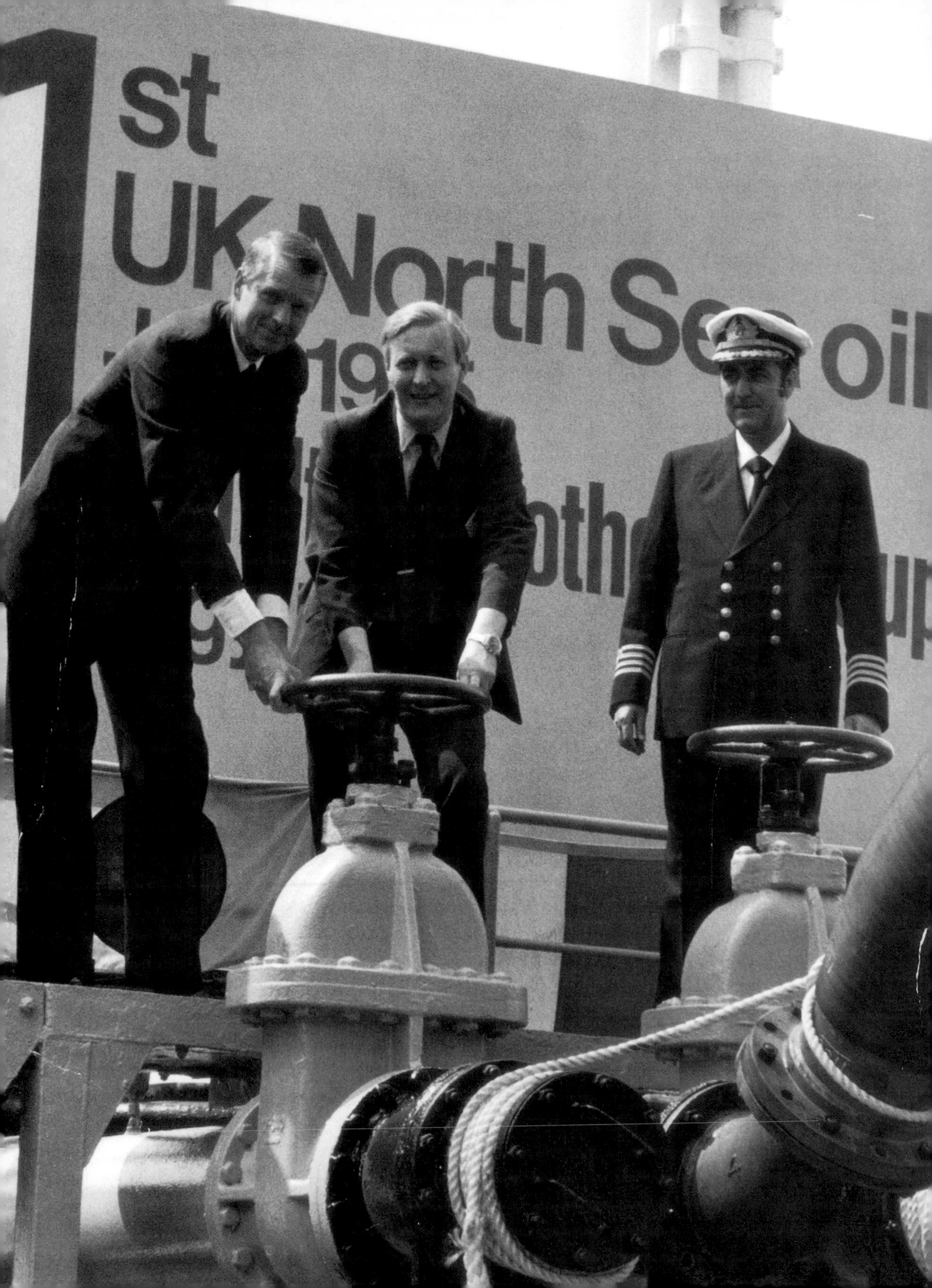
1
st
UK North
oil

parties alike, though this time it was a pleasant surprise for Labour. The Conservatives won 38 per cent of the vote, compared with Labour's 37 per cent, but Labour won more seats. The election left Labour with 301 seats, against the Tories with 297 and the Liberals on 14. For the second time since the war, the party with the largest share of the vote trailed in terms of seats.

With the result so close, Heath did not leave office immediately but first invited the Liberal leader Jeremy Thorpe to Number 10 to discuss the possibility of a coalition. This caused huge arguments within Liberal ranks as well as controversy in the country, and when the talks broke down Wilson was invited to Buckingham Palace to 'kiss hands'. Only four years after the surprise of defeat, Labour and Wilson were equally surprised to be back in office.

Despite being a minority administration, Wilson judged that the Liberals would support enough legislation to enable the party to func-tion as a government. Therefore, just as in 1964, he made no formal pacts and announced that he intended to govern as if he had a majority in the Commons.

Appointments in Harold Wilson's third administration were unsur-prising, with Denis Healey, former Defence Secretary, becoming the new Chancellor and James Callaghan the Foreign Secretary. Tony Crosland went to the Department of the Environment and Barbara Castle to Social Services. Tony Benn, who was increasingly veering to the left on all issues, went to Industry. With Shirley Williams as the new Secretary of State for Prices and Consumer Protection, Wilson's cabinet was the first ever in Britain to contain two women. And just as he had done in the 1960s, Wilson brought in a number of advisers to assist the policy-making process, though this time they were in a formalised Policy Unit.

The economic situation faced by the Labour government was one of the worst ever inheritances. In 1974 the balance of payments deficit rose to £3.3 billion and unemployment topped 600,000. Despite this, Wilson pressed on with a Queen's Speech containing increases in pensions, price controls and food subsidies. Within days of taking office, an agreement was also reached with the miners, bringing to an end the three-day week and state of emergency. Chancellor Healey introduced two budgets in 1974, an unusual step which reflected the state of economic crisis in Britain and in the wider world.

Tony Benn's first engagement as Energy Secretary in 1975 was the symbolic opening of the valve to start the flow of North Sea oil. 'I hold the future of Britain in my hand,' he said as he held aloft a bottle of crude oil. Oil and gas from the North Sea fields was a bonus for the British economy, and cushioned it in the balance of payments crises of the 1980s.

The election victory had also further strengthened the left's position within the party. Michael Foot, Tony Benn and Barbara Castle and other key figures on the left were in the cabinet, and in March 1974 the veteran left-winger Ian Mikardo was elected chair of the PLP. But the party was still united behind Wilson's leadership and the constraints imposed by the lack of a parliamentary majority meant that disagreements over Europe failed to resurface with their old virulence.

Even without a secure majority in the Commons, Labour still managed to pass many important and enduring pieces of legislation. In 1974 the Health and Safety at Work Act established a new commission to oversee working conditions. The Trade Union and Labour Relations Act 1974 repealed Heath's Industrial Relations Act, abolishing the National Industrial Relations Court. And a new Rent Act replaced the much resented 1972 Housing Finance Act which had replaced subsidised rent for council homes with 'fair rents'.

In September 1974 Wilson dissolved parliament and the second election in nine months was held on 10 October. Once again the political pundits were confounded, as the expected strong swing to Labour failed to materialise. Instead, Labour's share of the vote increased by only 2 per cent and the party won the narrowest of margins, a tiny five-seat majority in the House of Commons. The Tories lost 2 per cent and 22 seats, but the real losers in the election were the Liberals. Having put up the largest number of candidates in their history, hopeful of a real political breakthrough, they lost ground, winning a smaller share of the vote than in February and only 13 seats.

With Labour's parliamentary position at least strengthened, Wilson was now able to tackle the difficult issue of Europe. Foreign Secretary Callaghan had led the renegotiations of Britain's terms of entry during 1974, and at the Dublin meeting of the European Council in March 1975 Wilson obtained concessions on Britain's financial contribution to the Community. The government then put in place the measures necessary to hold a referendum on British membership of the Common Market. Wilson had already committed himself, in December 1974, to supporting the terms of entry if renegotiations were successful. However it was clear that the cabinet could not be held to collective responsibility on the issue. Therefore, while the government's position was to recommend support for continued European membership on the new terms, Wilson allowed members of the cabinet to take differing

OUT & INTO THE WORLD

OUT & INTO THE WORLD

public stances on the issue. In order to keep the party together, the cabinet had to be allowed to divide.

The Common Market referendum

Opposition to entry from within the cabinet came from left-wing members, such as Tony Benn and Barbara Castle, and, although they were in a minority in the cabinet, the wider party was similarly sceptical about Europe. The 1974 party conference voted against membership, and this decision was reiterated by a special conference in April 1975. But with the leadership of all three main political parties backing membership of the Community, supported by the bulk of the media, the 'No' campaign struggled to gain momentum. The result of the 1975 referendum was that over two-thirds were in favour of staying in the Common Market, a bigger majority than had been expected by either camp.

With Europe successfully dealt with, the Wilson government was still confronted by daunting economic problems. In July 1975 it published *The Attack on Inflation* proposing an across-the-board pay rise of a flat £6 a week for everyone earning under £8,500. But even with equitable pay restraint, inflation was still rising fast, while unemployment was also steadily growing. Despite this, the policies to control inflation and to sustain the 'social contract' appeared to be working. (The 'social contract', the government-union agreement for a 'social wage' in return for voluntary wage restraint, had replaced the 1972 Industrial Relations Act.) The number of strikes, which had rocketed under Heath's government, were also substantially reduced.

In March 1976, out of the blue, Wilson announced that he would be standing down as Prime Minister in three weeks' time. His decision threw the Labour Party into turmoil. There were six candidates in the battle for the succession: Benn, Foot, Jenkins, Callaghan, Healey and Crosland. Foot came top of the first poll, with 90 votes, but with other candidates eliminated or withdrawn, Callaghan won the contest on the third ballot with 176 votes to Foot's 137. The Wilson era was over.

In 1976 Harold Wilson made the surprise announcement of his resignation. There was a great deal of speculation over the reasons for his sudden departure, but Wilson had won four elections and was Labour's longest-serving Prime Minister. Jim Callaghan succeeded him as Labour Prime Minister.

The new Callaghan government brought with it some significant changes of personnel. Both Barbara Castle and Ted Short retired. Michael Foot replaced Short as Leader of the House, Crosland became Foreign Secretary, while Peter Shore went to Environment. Denis Healey remained as Chancellor of the Exchequer.

The economy was to dominate the life of the government. The day after Callaghan assumed office as Prime Minister, Healey introduced a budget which included £1.3 billion worth of tax cuts designed to revive the economy. Concern on the financial markets that Labour was borrowing to finance its election pledges led to a sterling crisis in 1976. Healey was forced to secure loans amounting to $3.5 billion from the International Monetary Fund combined with substantial cuts in public spending. But in general, the Labour administration dealt competently with a very difficult economic situation. The balance of payments, which had been in the red when Labour took over, was turned around to the extent that in 1977 there was a £53 million surplus, which grew to a massive £1,162 million surplus in 1978.

The difficult economic decisions made by the Wilson and Callaghan governments were not likely to pay quick electoral dividends. Labour's majority, which was tiny from the outset, was further reduced by a series of wounding by-election defeats. Defeats in Walsall North and Workington in November 1976, where 'safe' Labour seats were won by the Tories, emphasised the loss of popular support for the government. And when, in March 1977, the Conservatives put down a motion of censure in the Commons, the government only survived by agreeing a pact with the Liberal Leader David Steel. In return for Liberal support, Labour agreed to set up a Liberal-Labour Consultative Committee to examine proposals for legislation which both parties could support. The government's future was no longer in its own hands.

Apart from the economy, another major preoccupation of the government was devolution. Growing support for Scottish and Welsh nationalism in the 1960s and early 1970s had led Labour to put forward plans for assemblies in Scotland and Wales. However there was a substantial anti-devolution lobby within the Labour Party and, with its precarious parliamentary position, getting such difficult legislation through the Commons was fraught with difficulties and dangers. Opposition to the first Scotland and Wales Bill was such that it was talked out during its parliamentary stages. The government's second

The bitterly cold weather of the winter of 1978–79 made the shortages and privations caused by striking oil tanker and lorry drivers even harder for the public to bear. Police keeping an eye on pickets at an oil depot early in January (above) join them round their fire. Callaghan did not say, as appeared in one headline, 'Crisis? What crisis?', but the government seemed ineffectual.

attempt to pass legislation on devolution suffered damage from a series of disabling amendments, including a provision that a minimum of 40 per cent of the electorate in Scotland and Wales had to support devolution in a referendum if it was to go ahead. The results from the referendums, held on 1 March 1979 produced no majority for devolution in Wales, while in Scotland the small majority in favour did not exceed the 40 per cent threshold.

Callaghan's 'Winter of Discontent'

A series of crippling strikes also did great damage to the government's standing during the winter of 1978–79. Pay settlements for lorry drivers well above the 5 per cent recommendation led to a general collapse in the government's pay strategy and in January 1979 public sector workers, including ambulance drivers and dustmen, began strike action. The government managed to achieve a new agreement with the TUC, but by then the damage was already done. This 'Winter of Discontent'

Labour's Embattled Prime Minister

Fortified by that display of Liberal logic, the Opposition tabled their own vote of no confidence. We can only say that that once the Leader of the Opposition discovered what the Liberals and the SNP would do, she found the courage of their convictions. So, tonight, the Conservative Party, which wants the Act repealed and opposes even devolution, will march through the lobby with the SNP, which wants independence for Scotland, and with the Liberals, who want to keep the Act. What a massive display of unsullied principle!

The minority parties have walked into a trap. If they win, there will be a general election. I am told the current joke going around the House is that it is the first time in recorded history that turkeys have been known to vote for an early Christmas.

Jim Callaghan, 28 March 1979, in the House of Commons debate on the motion of no confidence, which resulted from the failure of the Devolution Acts was to cost Labour dear in electoral terms, more so even than Heath's U-turns and three-day week had done to the Conservatives in 1974.

With industrial strife widespread and plans for devolution killed off, the government was finally defeated on a vote of no confidence in the Commons on 28 March 1979. The margin could not have been narrower, 311 votes to 310, with a decisive abstention by two Irish Catholic MPs. The ensuing general election campaign saw the Conservatives on the offensive, now led by Margaret Thatcher. In increasingly strident and forceful language, the Tory campaign proclaimed that 'Labour isn't working'. The voters agreed and the result of the election was a clear victory for the Conservatives. Thatcher won almost 44 per cent of the vote, compared to Callaghan's 37 per cent and Steel's Liberals 14 per cent. This gave the Tories a large majority over the other parties and, more importantly, a clear mandate for their New Right platform of neo-liberal economics and a rolled-back state.

Labour's defeat in 1979 may seem in retrospect to have been inevitable, but this was not how it seemed at the time. In fact, after

The highly visible results of the strikes in the 'Winter of Discontent' made a dramatic impact. The heaps of festering garbage piled up in the streets and the pickets outside rubbish depots and hospitals lost the strikers public sympathy. 'Labour isn't Working' was a Tory slogan of the 1979 election campaign that followed.

Garland
– after –
Edward Lear

losing ground in the polls from April 1974 to November 1976, Labour's popularity with the voters increased during the second half of its term. By October 1977 it was back to level-pegging with the Tories at 45 per cent each and a year later Labour had opened up a five-point lead. If Prime Minister Callaghan had gone to the country in November 1978, as many in the party advised, the history of the Labour Party – and of the country – could have been very different.

In the event, the defeat intensified the divisions within the Labour Party. The left had been gradually building its strength throughout the 1970s. With the apparent failure of Keynesian-style economics, the right was ideologically weakened and its numbers depleted. Its leading figure, Roy Jenkins, had left parliament in 1977 to become a Commissioner in Europe, while the early death of Tony Crosland in 1977 had left a great void in the radical centre of the party. As the Conservatives moved to the right, so Labour quickened its march to the left. It was a time when the centre could not hold.

Yet Labour had achieved some notable legislative successes in government during the 1970s. Moreover the party had won four out of the five elections since 1964 and appeared to many to have become the natural party of government. The 1979 general election defeat was seen as a setback to this progress. The reality was that it marked the beginning of the long record of Conservative ascendancy and of Labour's agonised search for the road to renewal.

'Labour Left and Right battle it out' (above) a cartoon published in the *Telegraph* in 1979, has Healey and Benn spinning the Labour leader 'on his nose and his chin' like the Old Man of the West in Edward Lear's rhyme. After the 1979 defeat, deep divisions in the party surfaced once more.

Chapter Eight
Division and Renewal
1979–1992

The 1979 general election was not just a defeat for a political party. It was also the final burial of the post-war political consensus which had emerged out of Attlee's 1945 government and which had begun to fall apart during the 1970s. With her ideological mentors, New Right theorists such as Friedrich von Hayek and Milton Friedman, Mrs Thatcher was explicitly committed to breaking up this consensus. But within Labour's ranks, too, defeat encouraged demands for a more distinctly left-wing agenda. Tony Benn and his followers were as convinced as the Thatcherites that the old system had failed, although their prescription was radically different. It was a formula for political turmoil.

In the aftershock of defeat, James Callaghan managed to retain the leadership of the Labour Party without challenge. But the forces of the left, gathered and organised in the 1970s, were now ready for mobilisation. With key positions established on the National Executive Committee, and with a tightening grip on the constituency parties, the left soon set the agenda for Labour in opposition. Believing that the Labour government had not been radical enough, the left sought to change the party's constitution so that Labour Members of Parliament and Labour governments would have to be more responsive to the demands of the party's rank and file.

The rise of the left and splinters to the right

The first moves came at the 1979 party conference. After much argument, the conference agreed to make MPs face reselection during the life of every parliament. By doing this, it was believed that MPs would have to take greater account of party activists, who were largely left-wing, or face the threat of deselection. By the time of the 1983 election eight MPs had been deselected, almost all on the right of the party.

Old dissent was personified by Michael Foot, the Bevanite who became Labour leader in 1981, and new dissent by Tony Benn, the Gaitskellite who had moved to the left in the 1970s. Benn (sitting with Foot in the Commons, opposite) led the activists of the hard left in their bid to dominate Labour's policies after 1979.

The next constitutional battle was waged over the election of Labour's leaders. The Campaign for Labour Party Democracy and other hard-left pressure groups wanted the vote for the leadership to be taken out of the hands of the Parliamentary Party, which was felt to be dominated by the right, and transferred to an electoral college consisting of trade unions, MPs and constituency parties. With no clear decision on this made at the 1980 party conference, a special conference was proposed for January 1981 to consider it further.

But only days after the conference, Jim Callaghan announced his decision to step down as leader. It was thought that he had timed this carefully to enable his preferred successor to take over before any changes to the selection process had been agreed. Yet, even though the election took place under the old rules and with only the Parliamentary Party voting, this intention was to be frustrated. Four candidates stood: Peter Shore, Michael Foot, who had been deputy leader since 1976, John Silkin, who stood as a unity candidate, and former Chancellor Denis Healey. Healey was ahead on the first ballot, with 112 votes to Foot's 83, but after the withdrawal of Silkin and Shore, Foot came from behind to win by 139 votes to 129. Healey had to settle for the post of deputy leader.

Michael Foot, who was sixty-seven when he became leader of the Labour Party, was a veteran both of parliament and the left, with the old oratorial skills to match. But he was a dissident who, like his hero Nye Bevan, had gradually come in from the cold. He made valiant attempts to bring the party together, beginning with his victory speech when he quoted Bevan's words, 'Never underestimate the passion for unity in the Labour Party'. All the same, his election was seen by the public as a further lurch to the left by Labour.

At the special Wembley Conference on 24 January 1981, the party agreed to establish an electoral college for the election of its leader and deputy, made up of 40 per cent unions, 30 per cent Parliamentary Party and 30 per cent constituency parties. This decision, a victory for the left, precipitated the biggest crisis in the Labour Party's post-war history. On the day after the decision was taken, four former Labour cabinet ministers, Roy Jenkins, Shirley Williams, David Owen and William Rodgers, launched the Council for Social Democracy. The Council initially described itself as a pressure group within the party, but by the beginning of March twelve MPs had resigned the whip and indicated

The rise of the hard left caused the departure of the right. The 'Gang of Four' (David Owen, Bill Rodgers, Roy Jenkins and Shirley Williams, opposite) left the Labour Party in 1981 to form the SDP. Joined by a number of other MPs, their alliance with the Liberal Party challenged Labour for second place in the 1983 election.

The Limehouse Declaration:
The Formation of the Social Democratic Party
The conference disaster is the culmination of a long process by which the Labour Party has moved steadily away from its roots in the people of this country and its commitment to parliamentary government.

We propose to set up a Council for Social Democracy. Our intention is to rally all those who are committed to the values, principles and policies of social democracy...

We recognise that for those people who have given much of their lives to the Labour Party, the choice that lies ahead will be deeply painful. But we believe that the need for a realignment of British politics must now be faced.

The Limehouse Declaration, 25 January 1981

The riots in Liverpool's Toxteth area (above) were not the only inner-city disturbances that erupted in Britain in the summer of 1981. The Scarman report on the Brixton riots of the same year argued that unemployment and general social deprivation had contributed to the outbreaks of violent protest.

they would not stand as Labour candidates again. The formation of the Social Democratic Party (SDP) followed later the same month, boasting fourteen parliamentary recruits including one former Tory MP.

With the creation of the SDP it was crucial for Labour to restore stability within the party and achieve unity behind the new leader and his deputy. However, much to the anger of Foot and many of his parliamentary colleagues, Tony Benn announced in April 1981 that he would use the new election rules to challenge Healey for the post of deputy leader. With the party already in internal chaos, Benn's challenge inaugurated a period of open civil war. The election was due to take place on the eve of the October party conference, so the entire summer was spent in a damaging and often vicious election campaign. Adding to the controversy, many 'soft' left members of the Tribune Group, angered by Benn's decision to stand, announced publicly that they would not support him. Most notable of these was Neil Kinnock, the fiery MP for Bedwellty whose left-wing credentials were impeccable.

In the event, the result of the contest could not have been closer. On the first ballot, Healey secured 45 per cent, Benn 37 per cent and Silkin 18 per cent. On the second ballot, Healey won, though by less than one per cent. 'I had scraped in to victory by a hair of my eyebrow', Healey recorded in his memoirs. Abstention on the second vote by 18 Tribune members had been decisive in swinging the result in his favour. In defeat, Benn was unrepentant. Four days after the vote, he told his diary: 'I don't think we've done too badly at all, because this is a left that means to win, not a left that is prepared to make its point and lose and go along with another Wilson-type fudge; that isn't on.'

But there were two other effects of Benn's challenge. The first was an erosion of Labour's standing in the country, for it was clear to all that the party was fundamentally split between left and right. In a succession of by-elections, starting in Labour's heartland of Warrington, the new Social Democratic Party showed that it could challenge Labour in its own backyard. This was followed by a spectacular victory for Shirley Williams in the Conservative stronghold of Crosby, where a Tory majority of 18,000 was overturned by the SDP. Labour, divided and in disarray, found itself under threat even for the title of the official party of opposition.

The second effect was the splitting of the left itself, with the isolated 'hard' left being disowned by a growing 'soft' left group alarmed at what was happening to the party. At the 1981 party conference, the centre of the party was rallied and five left-wing members were defeated in the National Executive elections. Benn, though, remained characteristically unabashed and in December 1981 launched the Campaign Group as a rival on the left to the old Tribune group.

Thatcherism and the Falklands factor

Yet even with Labour tearing itself apart, the Conservative government had to struggle with its unpopularity with the electorate. Its New Right agenda had led to a dramatic rise in unemployment and there was mounting discontent both inside and and outside the Conservative Party over Margaret Thatcher's leadership. One dramatic impact of 'Thatcherism' was the outbreak of rioting in many inner city areas in July 1981. Lord Scarman, who reported on the Brixton riots, argued that unemployment, poor housing and inadequate education had created 'a predisposition towards violent protest' and recommended concerted action to improve conditions in Britain's inner cities.

Under growing pressure, Margaret Thatcher, announced her intention (unlike Heath before her) to plough on. 'You turn if you want to', she told the 1981 Conservative party conference, 'the Lady's not for turning'. Yet, the Conservatives remained behind in the polls for almost all of 1980 and 1981. Only Labour's internecine warfare brought any comfort. A poll in December 1981 made gloomy reading for both the main parties. The government and Labour both stood on 23 per cent, but the clear beneficiary of this common disillusionment was the SDP whose poll rating had rocketed to 50 per cent.

A dramatic event, however, was soon to come to the government's aid. On 2 April 1982, Argentinian troops invaded the Falkland Islands, a British territory in the South Atlantic. Parliament was recalled immediately, meeting on a Saturday, for a three-hour debate to discuss the crisis. The House was united in its response, with Mrs Thatcher getting the support of the Labour leader Michael Foot, who not only attacked the Argentine Junta (the right-wing military regime) but also demanded strong action from the government. The government's immediate response was to despatch a Task Force to the South Atlantic while also seeking to apply diplomatic pressure on Argentina. The military stand-off was broken on 1 May, and the following day, a British submarine sank the *General Belgrano,* an Argentine cruiser, with the loss of over three hundred lives.

Any idea of a cross-party consensus was shattered on 20 May, when 33 Labour MPs voted against the government's handling of the war, a move that was condemned by Michael Foot as stabbing British troops in the back. But while this vote was taking place in Westminster, British troops were landing on East Falkland to begin the battle to win back the islands. Within a week, British forces had succeeded in winning control of the main island with relatively few casualties, and the final recapture of Port Stanley, the Falklands' capital, took place on 14 June. The whole conflict had cost over two hundred British and seven hundred Argentinian lives. With victory achieved, the war became a political prize for the Conservatives and Mrs Thatcher, and it was eagerly exploited. The 'Iron Lady' came into her own. From a low point of 23 per cent in the polls, Conservative support rose to 41.5 per cent in May 1982 and reached 46.5 per cent by July.

By contrast, just as Mrs Thatcher was gaining a reputation as a strong leader, Michael Foot's leadership qualities were coming in for increasing censure. Foot's personal appearance, symbolised by his 'donkey' jacket at the Cenotaph, was a source of particular criticism. In addition, he was

British troops received a heroes' welcome when they came home from their victory in the 1982 Falklands war (opposite). Margaret Thatcher, whose domestic policies had been under attack, was now admired as a strong national leader. She was turning the title 'the Iron Lady' (originally a Soviet accusation) into an accolade.

The women's Peace Camp at Greenham Common was set up in 1981 outside the American base to protest against Cruise nuclear missiles. In 1982 thousands of women (above) linked hands in an 'embrace of the base'. Unilateral disarmament became a party issue when activists on the left succeeded in making it a part of the 1983 Labour manifesto.

presented as old, weak and a prisoner of the left, attacks which further undermined Labour's already poor electoral position.

Yet the general election of May 1983 was even more a battle of ideologies than of leaders. Labour's manifesto contained proposals for massive public investment, withdrawal from the EEC, abolition of the House of Lords, unilateral nuclear disarmament and renationalisation of any industry privatised by the government. It was the most explicitly left-wing programme that the party had ever adopted, dubbed 'the longest suicide note in history' by one shadow cabinet member.

Having focused much of its energies during the previous years to internal debates and constitutional matters, the party went into the election poorly prepared and with no clear media strategy. Its membership had also declined sharply. Having stood at over 650,000 in 1979, in one year this figure had almost halved, and by 1981 it had further slumped to around 250,000.

The result of the election, although still a shock to party members, was never in doubt. The Conservatives won a landslide victory, taking

397 seats and extending their majority over all other parties to 144. The real battle of the election was for second place between the Liberal/Social Democratic Party Alliance and Labour. The Alliance won 25.4 per cent of the vote, only a whisker behind Labour, who gained 27.6 per cent, the party's lowest showing since 1918.

The stark fact was that Labour had come perilously close to being replaced as the main opposition. The political abyss had beckoned. The only ray of hope came from the fact that, while they had won a huge number of seats, the Tories had not increased their share of the vote. Indeed at 42.4 per cent, they had won with a smaller share of the vote than for any post-war Conservative government. But this offered little comfort in Labour's desperate plight.

After the 1983 defeat, Michael Foot resigned as party leader. With Tony Benn ruled out after losing his own seat, the left lacked credible candidates in the contest for the succession. The overwhelming victor was Neil Kinnock, who won 71 per cent of the votes in the electoral college, including 92 per cent of constituency votes and almost three-quarters of union support. The much-heralded 'dream team' was completed when Roy Hattersley, Shadow Home Secretary from 1981 and on the centre-right of the party, was elected as deputy.

Unemployment reached the three-million mark in the recession of 1982, and people were again marching for jobs (below) as the 1983 election campaign was being fought. Labour was promising considerable public investment and the renationalisation of industries that had been privatised.

The miner's strike, Militant and Kinnock's modernisation of the party

Kinnock immediately sought to restore unity within the party. At the 1983 Conference he deployed all his eloquence to emphasise the need to beat the Tories rather than fight each other: 'They are the enemy: they must be defeated, and we must defeat them together. If we try by groups and factions, we will not do it. If we give greater attention to arguments between ourselves than to our enmity against them, we will not do it. If we give more attention to impressing each other than convincing the people we have to convince, we will not do it.'

But unity was easier to proclaim than achieve. Before Kinnock had time to move the party forward, he was forced on to the defensive by a major industrial dispute. In March 1984, the majority of coal mines across Britain were shut by strike action, with miners rejecting a pay offer and protesting about threatened pit closures. The strike was effective across almost all of the country outside Nottinghamshire, despite the fact that it was not backed by a national strike ballot and was called at an unpropitious time at the end of the winter.

The dispute posed problems for Kinnock and the Labour Party. The miners were traditionally seen as Labour heroes, and were still a powerful force within the party; there was widespread sympathy for their position, not least in Kinnock's own South Wales heartlands. The history of the miners' defeat in 1926 was not forgotten. But the miners' leader Arthur Scargill was regarded by the Labour leadership as misguided and sectarian. With the press and the Conservative Party goading Kinnock to condemn the picket-line violence and lack of strike ballot, the Labour leader had a rough ride. But he roundly condemned all violence and sought to separate support for the miners from endorsement of the actions of Scargill.

The 1984 party conference revealed the mammoth task facing Kinnock in transforming the Labour Party. In addition to the attacks over his stance on the miners' strike, the leadership's proposals to change the selection process for parliamentary candidates to One Member, One Vote, seen as a threat by the left, were defeated. The conference also passed a motion proposed by Derek Hatton, Leader of Liverpool City Council and prominent member of the far-left 'entryist' group, the Militant Tendency. Hatton called for support for the action of councils, including his own, which broke the law in the face of Tory

The disaster of the 1983 election left Labour's new leader Neil Kinnock with the gigantic task of turning the party away from its internal battles to present a united front against Thatcherism. With Glenys Kinnock (opposite), he acknowledges the standing ovation for his first conference speech as leader in 1984.

'rate-capping' (in 1984 the Thatcher government had set legally binding limits to the amount that local councils could raise from the rates). With Militant's numbers in the party swelling, there was doubt whether the considerable task of rescuing the Labour Party from itself was even possible.

But only one year later, with the miners defeated, Kinnock saw his chance to begin the battle in earnest against the extremists and factions that he knew were so damaging to the party's standing with the electorate. His opportunity came through the activities of the Militant-controlled Liverpool City Council. Its policy of budget over-spending had led to a financial crisis, and only days before the conference Derek Hatton had ordered the issuing of redundancy notices to all council officers, delivered by a fleet of hired taxis.

Neil Kinnock's conference speech was a devastating response. After attacking the Conservative failures on employment and welfare, Labour's leader rounded on Militant, vigorously denouncing the kind of politics it represented:

I'll tell you what happens with impossible promises. You start with far-fetched resolutions. They are pickled into a rigid dogma, a code, and you go through the years sticking to that, out-dated, misplaced, irrelevant to the real needs, and you end in the grotesque chaos of a Labour council – a Labour council – hiring taxis to scuttle round a city handing out redundancy notices to its own workers. I am telling you, no matter how entertaining, how fulfilling to short-term egos – I'm telling you and you'll listen – you can't play politics with people's jobs and with people's services or with their homes.

During this speech, Kinnock was heckled by Militant supporters, including Hatton himself, who walked out while Kinnock was still speaking. The Liverpool MP Eric Heffer also stormed off the party platform. But most of the party delegates applauded Kinnock's passion and his assault on Militant. It was clearly a decisive moment. The *Guardian* described it as 'the bravest and most important speech by a Labour Leader in over a generation'.

But there was more to come. On the very next day, Kinnock took the unusual and courageous step of responding himself to a motion, proposed by Scargill, calling for a Labour government to refund any money lost by unions as a result of strike action. On the back of his attack on Militant, Kinnock took the opportunity to castigate the

The miners' strike of 1984 (opposite) began with the Yorkshire miners coming out in protest at the Cortonwood colliery closure. It ended in an even worse defeat than the 1926 strike of bitter memory. Coal was no longer 'King' in British industry and the Thatcher government was prepared and eager for a ruthless and decisive confrontation with a major union.

The Militant-controlled Liverpool City Council, headed by Derek Hatton (above), was one of Kinnock's targets at the 1985 conference. In his passionate assault on the hard left, Kinnock also took on NUM leader Arthur Scargill with a scathing attack on his tactics during the miners' strike.

miners' leader and his tactics. Taking apart one by one the arguments for reimbursement, Kinnock spoke of a miner in his Welsh constituency who had complained that the strike had been called without a ballot, at the end of winter, and in the face of a hostile government. How could this happen? Kinnock's miner said it happened 'because nobody really thought it out'. In the course of a single conference, Kinnock had taken on the two bastions of left-wing sectarianism: Militant and Arthur Scargill. It was the defining moment of his early leadership and a turning-point for the whole party.

After the conference, an investigation was launched into the activities of Militant in Liverpool, resulting in the expulsion of Hatton and many of his colleagues from the Labour Party. These expulsions were opposed by the hard left, but gained support from an increasingly large soft-left section of the party, including David Blunkett, the Sheffield Council leader, and Michael Meacher, former Bennite who now had spurned the Campaign Group. With the support of such figures, Kinnock was also successful at winning back control of the National Executive Committee and key policy committees. In the run-up to the general election, many policies which were associated with the defeat in 1983 were changed or dropped. Opposition to the sale of council houses was dropped, as was a commitment to withdraw from the European Community. On union legislation, the party was still locked into repealing Conservative legislation, but would itself force unions to hold strike ballots and elect officers.

Modernisation of the party's style and presentation was also clearly needed and in 1985 a new Campaigns and Communications directorate was created. The new organisation, under the guidance of Peter Mandelson, the grandson of Herbert Morrison and an experienced media figure, was to transform the party's public image. Mandelson commissioned professional consultants to report on the state of the party and to undertake qualitative research into the views of target voters. They reported that the Labour Party was associated too closely with minority groups, with an out-dated cloth cap image and with some deeply unpopular policies. The party's response was to focus its campaigning on positive issues, such as the NHS, and to try to neutralise negative issues like defence. At the 1986 conference, the Labour Party also adopted a new emblem, the red rose, which replaced the red flag and was designed to symbolise Labour's modernisation.

Early in 1986 the Conservative government began to look distinctly vulnerable. There was a bitter row over the future of the Westland helicopter company between Minister of Defence Michael Heseltine and Trade Secretary Leon Brittan. Papers were leaked that were critical of Heseltine, Thatcher's style of government was at issue and both Heseltine and Brittan resigned in January, the former in anger, the latter pressured to go. Labour was ahead in the polls and made substantial gains in the May municipal elections, also winning a by-election in Fulham.

But despite Labour's revival and the problems in the Conservative camp, as the election drew nearer the old problems on central issues such as defence continued to trouble Labour. Just days before the party's 1986 conference, the US Defence Secretary Caspar Weinberger told a BBC

Early in 1986 the Thatcher government was rocked by the row over the future of the Westland helicopter company. It led to the resignations of Leon Brittan and Michael Heseltine (the latter shown with Margaret Thatcher on the cover of *Private Eye*, below).

Labour

Labour's new emblem, the red rose, is displayed behind the platform at the 1986 conference. Under Neil Kinnock and Roy Hattersley as leader and deputy leader (on the right, above), modernisation was changing Labour's substance as well as its style. The party's programme for the 1987 election was to be very different from its 1983 manifesto.

television programme that Labour's defence plans could lead to the break up of NATO. The Conservative Party propaganda machine went into top gear. Kinnock made two visits to the United States, seeking to emphasise how the two countries would remain closely linked under Labour, but this only served to highlight Labour's unpopular plans to scrap Polaris and Trident (submarine-launched nuclear missiles). On his second visit, Kinnock was snubbed by President Reagan who set aside only thirty minutes to talk to him. This was in marked contrast to the treatment Mrs Thatcher received on her visit to the Soviet Union the following week, where she was greeted as a great international leader.

When the general election was announced for 11 June 1987, Labour strategists tried to turn the poll into a presidential-style election in which Kinnock was presented as an orator and man of the people. On 15 May, at the Welsh Labour Party conference, Kinnock delivered his famous 'Why am I the first Kinnock in a thousand generations to get to university' speech, a piece of high emotion which moved many of his

The First Kinnock in a Thousand Generations...

Why am I the first Kinnock in a thousand generations to be able to get to university? Was it because all our predecessors were 'thick'? Did they lack talent – those people who could sing, and play, and recite poetry; those people who could make wonderful, beautiful things with their hands; those people who could dream dreams, see visions; those people who had such a sense of perception as to know in times so brutal, so oppressive, that they could win their way out of that by coming together?

Were those people not university material? Couldn't they have knocked off their A-levels in an afternoon? But why didn't they get it? Was it because they were weak – those people who could work eight hours a day underground and then come up and play football? Those women who could survive eleven child-bearings, were they weak? Those people who could stand with the backs and legs straight and face the great – the people who had control over their lives, the ones that owned their workplaces and tried to own them – and tell them 'No, I won't take your orders.' Were they weak? Does anybody really think that they didn't get what we had because they didn't have the talent, or the strength, or the endurance, or the commitment? Of course not. It was because there was no platform on which they could stand.

Neil Kinnock, speech to the Annual Conference of the Welsh Labour Party, 15 May 1987, just before the general election audience to tears. This was followed by a party political broadcast focused entirely on Kinnock himself, made by the director of the film *Chariots of Fire* Hugh Hudson; this improved Kinnock's image as leader, and was widely recognised as a presentational success. It did something to counteract the damage caused to the party by the hostile, often exaggerated press stories about the 'loony Labour left', the London councils controlled by the hard left in the 1980s.

Yet Labour's strategists were realistic about the goals for the party during the campaign: these were to displace the Alliance and re-establish Labour's position. Privately there was no real expectation of victory. The defence issue in particular haunted the campaign and was relentlessly exploited by the Tories. During an interview with David Frost, in the face of repeated questioning about Labour's non-nuclear defence policy, Kinnock seemed to say that guerilla warfare would be Labour's response to a Soviet attack on Britain. The Tories seized on the political opportunities presented by Labour's defence policy, claiming that Labour was waving the red flag of socialism and the white flag of surrender. The final week of the campaign saw the appearance of Conservative posters, headlined as Labour's defence policy, showing a picture of a surrendering soldier with both hands in the air.

The recovery from the 1987 election defeat

While defeat was not unexpected, the scale of Labour's defeat was deeply demoralising. Despite having largely won the campaign, Labour lost the election heavily, finishing with only 31.7 per cent of the vote and 229 seats. The Conservatives won 376 seats, 21 less than in 1983 but still enough to give them a healthy majority. Labour did, however, succeed in seeing off the Alliance, which took 23.2 per cent of the vote and only 22 seats. The defeat made clear the extent to which the public feared Labour, and how much work remained to be done to make the party electable again.

The first period of Kinnock's leadership turned out to be merely a rehearsal for the more fundamental changes that were to come after the 1987 defeat. Led initially by Tom Sawyer, the former Bennite and deputy general secretary of the public service union NUPE, who chaired the Home Policy sub-committee on the NEC, leading party figures called for a review both of Labour's policies and of its basic aims and values.

The 1987 party conference passed a motion calling for a Policy Review, an initiative backed by Kinnock who used his speech to criticise those who had 'do not disturb' notices attached to their minds. The conference also supported changes to the candidate selection process, which Kinnock had tried unsuccessfully to change in 1984. Instead of selection by general committees of constituency Labour parties, the new plans put selection in the hands of an electoral college containing affiliated organisations and constituencies.

With a Policy Review in hand, Kinnock and Hattersley came in for criticism from the left for their style of leadership. While the soft left were still supportive, the hard-left Campaign Group believed the Policy Review amounted to the ditching of socialism, 'the Thatcherisation of the Labour Party' as Benn put it, and believed that Kinnock's leadership should be challenged. After much speculation, the Campaign Group therefore nominated Tony Benn as leader and Eric Heffer as deputy. John Prescott, MP for Hull and former seaman, also threw his hat into the ring against Hattersley, angered at the way he thought he had been sidelined by the deputy leader.

As in 1981, this leadership challenge caused instability within the party and diverted attention from the campaign against Thatcherism. But this time the result was not close. Kinnock won 88 per cent in the electoral college, with Benn getting the support of only 38 MPs and less than one in six of the constituencies. The battle for deputy leader was also won decisively by Hattersley, with two-thirds of the vote, against Prescott's 23 per cent and Heffer's 9 per cent. Far from weakening his position, the challenge from the Campaign Group had succeeded in strengthening Kinnock's direction of the party. Even Benn acknowledged that for the left the result was appalling.

Further moves towards modernisation followed. The principle of One Member, One Vote for future elections to the National Executive Committee was approved, while the party's membership system was transformed by the introduction of a national membership scheme, with all the information held centrally on a computer in Labour's headquarters at Walworth Road in London. The policy-making process was also extended by the approval of plans for a National Policy Forum, where elected members could undertake a more detailed and coherent discussion of party policy than was allowed by the 'resolutionary socialist' approach of party conference.

In 1988 there appeared the first fruits of the Policy Review, in the form of a paper entitled *Democratic Socialism: Aims and Values*. Written largely by Roy Hattersley, it reflected the deputy leader's view of socialism as the means for practical freedom for individuals. After the ideological warfare that had dogged the party for so long, this paper was seen as an important step in redefining what democratic socialism was essentially about.

The following year saw the completion of the Policy Review process with the publication of *Meet the Challenge, Make the Change*. The document was a cornerstone of Kinnock's revisionism. It contained a reversal of Labour's commitment to unilateralism, a policy of fair taxation with no return to high marginal rates of income tax, and a rejection of old-style nationalisation with no pledge to renationalise privatised utilities. The document also recorded the virtues of the market, while recognising its deficiencies and weaknesses. In one passage which reflected the German Social Democratic Party's 1959 Bad Godesberg programme, *Meet the Challenge, Make the Change* proclaimed that the role of government was 'to help make the market system work properly when it can, will and should – and to replace or strengthen it where it can't, won't or shouldn't'.

The Policy Review documents were attacked by the left as further evidence of the party's adaptation to Thatcherism and betrayal of socialism. The whole process of modernisation also came under attack from assorted quarters, including the TGWU leader, Ron Todd, who famously criticised sharp-suited socialists with filofaxes and mobile phones. But in reality the Policy Review owed as much to the work of Crosland and earlier revisionists as it did to the new world created by Margaret Thatcher. Labour had taken stock of the kind of party it was, or at least wanted to be.

Neil Kinnock's revisionism was remarkably successful. The Labour Party's aims and values had been clarified, unpopular policies abandoned, the party's organisation strengthened, and sectarianism confronted. Membership had also begun to grow again, and Kinnock had been able to mobilise the affections and loyalties of ordinary party members against the extremes. This was confirmed by the defeat of Ken Livingstone, former leader of the Greater London Council (which had been disbanded under Thatcher) and vocal critic of Kinnock, in the elections for the NEC in 1989.

Democratic Socialism:
The Creation of a Genuinely Free Society

The true purpose of democratic socialism and, therefore, the true aim of the Labour Party, is the creation of a genuinely free society, in which the fundamental objective of government is the protection and extension of individual liberty irrespective of class, sex, age, race, colour or creed. Socialists understand that the rights of that free society can only have real meaning for men and women who possess the economic and political strength to exercise them. To socialists, freedom is much more than the absence of restraint or the assertion of the rudimentary rights of citizenship. Protection from coercion – by state, corporate or private power of every sort – is only the first step towards liberty. When so many men and women cannot afford to make the choices which freedom provides, the idea that all enjoy equal and extensive liberty is a deception. Unless men and women have the power to choose, the right to choose has no value.

Democratic Socialism: Aims and Values, The Labour Party, 1988

The crisis of Thatcherism: the campaign of 1992

While Labour's unity and popularity was growing, the Conservatives were losing electoral support and engaging in internal battles of their own. As signs of recession appeared in the late 1980s, there was a mounting sense that the Conservative economic 'miracle' had been a mirage. Disillusionment with the government's handling of the economy quickly turned into electoral unpopularity, seen in the result of the 1989 European elections. Labour gained some spectacular by-election victories, including a historic 21 per cent swing and majority of 10,000 in the 'safe' Tory seat of Mid-Staffordshire.

There were also signs of strong Tory disagreements over Europe. In November 1989 Chancellor Nigel Lawson finally resigned after comments by Mrs Thatcher's adviser Sir Alan Walters on the Exchange Rate Mechanism. This was followed by dissension over the introduction of the deeply disliked Community Charge, or Poll Tax, in April 1990. Many Tory backbenchers were extremely concerned at the new local tax, which was unpopular because it was levied on all individuals regardless of their ability to pay, and showed every sign of being a political time-bomb. Mrs Thatcher remained characteristically defiant, even claiming that 'the Community Charge will be very popular', but a massive public demonstration in London against the Poll Tax on the eve of its launch signalled the trouble ahead.

It came, thick and fast, and from different directions. On 1 November 1990 the Deputy Prime Minister, Geoffrey Howe, resigned from the government over Mrs Thatcher's negative stance on Europe. His resignation speech in the Commons two days later was devastating, with its description of Mrs Thatcher's approach to Europe in terms of 'sending your opening batsmen to the crease only for them to find...that their bats have been broken before the game by the team captain.' With the government in disarray, former cabinet minister and Thatcher adversary, Michael Heseltine, launched a leadership challenge. Mrs Thatcher was forced to resign on 22 November 1990, after eleven and a half years as Prime Minister, replaced by her Chancellor John Major, who beat Heseltine and Foreign Secretary Douglas Hurd. The political situation was suddenly transformed, but it was at Labour's expense. A government had been changed, an unpopular leader deposed, but without a general election. Labour was entitled to feel cheated.

In 1990 there were Poll Tax riots in London's Trafalgar Square (above) and serous disturbances all over the country. After Margaret Thatcher had been deposed over this and other differences with her ministers, the Poll Tax was scrapped.

John Major became Prime Minister on the eve of the Gulf War. Iraq had invaded Kuwait and Britain joined the USA and other allies in sending troops to the Gulf to do battle to free Kuwait. Except for a small number of MPs, the Labour Party condemned the actions of Iraq and supported the government's response. While there was no direct re-run of the 'Falklands factor', the conflict raised the profile of the new Prime Minister. The Government's poll ratings improved somewhat in 1991, as John Major scrapped the Poll Tax and tried to distance himself from the more unpopular elements of Thatcherism. By the time of the general election in April 1992, the outcome seemed too close to call.

After the professionalism of 1987, Labour's 1992 campaign had much to live up to. In many ways, it failed miserably. While defence was no longer a contentious issue, taxation certainly was. John Smith, the Shadow Chancellor, produced a 'shadow' budget early in the campaign in an effort to prevent the expected campaign of misinformation about

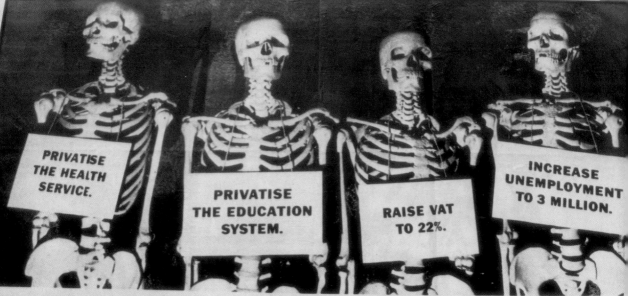

PRIVATISE
THE HEALTH
SERVICE.

PRIVATISE
THE EDUCATION
SYSTEM.

RAISE VAT
TO 22%.

INCREASE
UNEMPLOYMENT
TO 3 MILLION.

How many more have the Tories got in their cupboard?

Labou

'IF THE TORIES
HAD A SOUL
THEY'D SELL IT'

Labour's tax plans. In fact, this exercise had precisely the opposite effect. With the Tory tabloids, Tory broadcasts and national poster campaigns all claiming that Labour's 'double whammy' on tax would cost every family £1,000 extra a year, Labour's own claim that four out of five families would gain under their plans was lost in the barrage.

Labour's strongest card was the National Health Service, but even this was turned into a source of embarrassment as a result of an election broadcast ('Jennifer's ear' as it became known) after the details of the real child on whom the broadcast was loosely based were leaked to the press. There was also the problem of Kinnock's judgment as leader, which was highlighted by his prematurely triumphant performance at a mass election rally in Sheffield, an event widely credited with damaging the public perception of both the party and its leader.

As the day of the election approached, the hostility of the Tory press to the Labour Party, and particularly Neil Kinnock's leadership, intensified. The *Sun*, with the biggest circulation in Britain, led the way on the day before the election, in its eight-page feature about the 'Nightmare on Kinnock Street'. This was followed on April 9 by the front-page headline: 'If Kinnock wins today, will the last person in Britain please turn out the lights.' But while the *Sun* was the most outrageous, it was by no means alone. Almost all the tabloid newspapers ran a series of scare stories about Labour throughout the election. It was a negative press campaign almost unprecedented in British political history.

Just before midnight on 9 April, amid expectation that Labour would win with a narrow majority, the result from Basildon was announced. This key marginal seat had been held by the Conservatives. For Labour supporters across the country a night that had begun with such hope and optimism after so many years in the wilderness had ended in tears. Labour achieved only a 2 per cent swing and gained 271 seats to the Tories' 336. John Major had held on with a slim 21-seat majority.

At 5.30 am on 10 April, outside Labour's Walworth Road headquarters, Neil Kinnock spoke to waiting reporters and party members: 'I naturally feel a strong sense of disappointment, not for myself, for I am very fortunate in my personal life, but I feel dismay and sorrow for so many people in our country who do not share this personal good fortune. They deserve better than they got on 9 April 1992. The whole country deserves better.' Labour's long road to renewal had ended in another cul-de-sac.

This Labour poster for the 1992 election (opposite, above), exploits anxieties over some aspects of the New Right ideology. A slogan in the same campaign (opposite, below) recalls Harold Macmillan's warning in the 1980s that the Tories were in danger of 'selling off the family silver' in their enthusiasm for privatisation.

Chapter Nine
New Labour, New Party
1992–today

Its fourth election defeat in a row was a devastating blow to Labour. Once again the question was asked whether the party could ever recover from the loss. Within days of the defeat, Neil Kinnock quickly announced his intention to stand down and make way for a new leader. The obvious successor was John Smith, the fifty-four year old Shadow Chancellor. A Scottish lawyer, who had become a very effective parliamentarian, Smith had been first elected in 1970 and was the youngest member of the cabinet in the last years of the Callaghan government. He had suffered a heart attack in 1988, but still enjoyed his favourite pastime of walking the Munros in the Scottish highlands.

Smith was challenged for the leadership by Bryan Gould, a New Zealander by birth, who had been elected for Dagenham in 1983 and had been an important figure in Kinnock's reformed Labour Party. Gould also stood in the contest for deputy leader, with John Prescott and Margaret Beckett as the other candidates.

When the results were announced at a special conference in July, John Smith was the emphatic victor, with 91 per cent of the votes in the electoral college, including 29.3 per cent out of a possible 30 per cent in the constituency section. Gould was also beaten in the contest for deputy leader, which Margaret Beckett won convincingly with almost 58 per cent against Gould's 15 per cent and John Prescott's 28 per cent.

Smith had been elected on a platform of continued modernisation of the party. His campaign programme, *New Paths to Victory,* called for a radical response to the four election defeats, including the reform of the trade union block vote. In his acceptance speech, he also proclaimed that if the party was to convince the electorate of its democratic credentials, it must begin by reforming itself.

When parliament began its new session after the election, there was also a historic change to the House of Commons. For the first time in

John Smith was elected as Labour's new leader in 1992 as a moderniser. In his acceptance speech he made it clear that, after four election defeats, Labour would be unlikely to get into power until it had reformed itself. Beside him stands Margaret Beckett, the new deputy leader.

British history, MPs elected a woman as Speaker of the House of Commons – Betty Boothroyd, a Labour MP since 1973 and Deputy Speaker from 1987. Her inimitable style, tough, yet humorous and fair-minded, was to win her many friends on all sides of the House over the coming years.

The party's voting systems are revised

Labour's new process of modernisation began at its 1992 party conference. The trade union share of conference votes was reduced from 90 per cent to 70 per cent. In his conference speech, Smith also hinted at the reform of parliamentary selections to One Member, One Vote,

and set out his vision of Labour in government, an approach which he described as using the power of all to help promote individual success. He was supported by other prominent modernisers who had been elected to the Shadow Cabinet in 1992. These included Smith's younger Scottish ally, Gordon Brown, and Tony Blair, the MP for Sedgefield, who shared Smith's profound belief in a politics based on strong Christian values. Coming first and second in the shadow cabinet poll, Brown was appointed Shadow Chancellor, a role that he had performed temporarily in 1988 after John Smith's heart attack, while Blair became Shadow Home Secretary.

But Smith's honeymoon period as leader soon came to an end. By 1993 it was apparent that there were rumblings of discontent over several issues. In part, it was a question of the style of leadership. Smith was a team player, always anxious to ensure that he took his colleagues along with him. This brought a reluctance to lead from the front, a weakness that some found irritating. There was in addition criticism over his approach to the reform of the Labour Party. Those who wanted to move faster and further claimed that Smith was 'sleepwalking into oblivion', seeming to believe that with only minor adjustments Labour would be able to win the next election. By contrast, radical modernisers argued that the party needed much more fundamental reforms if it was ever to be electable again.

This view was supported by an internal party report into the 1992 election defeat (called 'What the Electorate Think of Us') produced in early 1993. This suggested that, despite Conservative unpopularity, the electorate had no clear idea what Labour stood for, creating a vacuum in which negative attacks from the Tories were too easily believed. The party had lost the 1992 election, not because of short-term factors such as the Sheffield rally, the 'Jennifer's ear' episode or even because of the negative press campaign, but because of deep-seated doubts and fears about Labour's identity and programme. The message was clear: if Labour was ever to win the trust of the electorate again, nothing less than a radical remaking of the party would be enough.

There were some on the traditional left who drew different conclusions about the change of direction that was required, arguing that the lesson of defeat was that the party should put forward a clear socialist agenda, including the return of privatised utilities to public ownership and higher taxation. Reports that modernisers such as Brown and Blair

Betty Boothroyd (opposite) became Speaker of the House of Commons in 1992, the first time a woman had been chosen. A professional dancer in her young days, she had worked as political assistant to Labour ministers and entered parliament herself in 1973. Her political experience and Yorkshire firmness and humour have brought her great admiration and respect.

had been to the United States to talk to Clinton's campaign aides after the Democrats' presidential victory in November 1992 seemed to the left to be proof that Labour was abandoning its traditional roots.

It was against this background that Smith launched his campaign to introduce One Member, One Vote (OMOV) for the selection of parliamentary candidates. Smith's plans had already received a setback when the 1992 conference voted to keep the union vote at all levels of the party. Undeterred, Smith began discussions with key unions and the constituency parties, outlining his plans for change. The proposals, which removed direct union representation in parliamentary selections, were central in projecting the image that Smith wanted for Labour – as an independent party which was not in the pockets of the union 'barons'. The reforms would also extend democracy within the party by allowing every member to take part in candidate selection ballots.

With the 1993 conference drawing near, it was clear that the vote on this reform package was on a knife-edge. Facing a possible defeat, Smith raised the stakes by making it clear that he would resign as leader if he lost. In the event, One Member, One Vote was approved by a margin of 3.2 per cent, but only because of the abstention of the Manufacturing Science and Finance trade union and the extraordinary last-minute speech from John Prescott who had been asked to speak by Smith only hours before the ballot – his influence with grass-roots activists was seen as crucial in swinging the vote. But having won the narrowest of victories on this issue, Smith then received a clear message from conference on any future change when it passed a motion defending Clause IV of the party's constitution.

The election defeat brought further changes for the party. It focused attention on the issue of electoral reform. Labour had tried to woo Liberal Democrat voters in the last week of the 1992 campaign with talk of possible changes in the voting system, and in the aftermath of defeat there were calls from some quarters for a Lab-Lib pact and a commitment to electoral reform. John Smith preferred to put the issue in the hands of a party commission, headed by Professor Raymond Plant. In the event, the final Plant Report was ambiguous in its recommendations, settling on a compromise system of 'supplementary' voting which Plant himself did not support. John Smith resolved the dilemma by proposing that any future reforms of the system should be put to a national referendum.

THE LAST WALTZ

~ ©Steve Bell 1993 ~   ~ 328·30·9·93 ~

Another change turned on the role of women within the party. Despite fielding 134 women candidates in the general election, only 35 were elected, in part because many women were selected for constituencies that Labour had little hope of winning. To ensure that more women would be elected, the 1992 Labour Party conference approved a motion calling for all-women shortlists in a percentage of key marginal seats and in Labour seats where MPs were retiring. The party also agreed to introduce a women's section in the constituency ballot for elections to the National Executive. In 1993 this resulted in the NEC having a strong representation of women, including Harriet Harman and Clare Short.

John Smith moves to extract Labour from the embrace of the TUC cart-horse with the Last Waltz modernised into the Twist, in this cartoon by Steve Bell. By a narrow margin, the 1993 conference approved One Member, One Vote in the selection of parliamentary candidates, removing the union block votes.

Black Wednesday, political scandals and the Tory defeat on Maastricht

The Conservatives had won a fourth consecutive election victory, but their standing was rapidly eroded by a series of crises, scandals and rebellions. The first disaster came on 16 September 1992 when speculation against the pound led to the government spending over two billion pounds in what proved to be an ultimately fruitless battle to defend sterling. Britain was forced to withdraw from the European Exchange Rate Mechanism (ERM); but this Black Wednesday was to be only the first of many black days for the Major government.

The handling of the crisis was seen as hapless. Chancellor Norman Lamont announced that he had been 'singing in the bath' on the night of the economic crisis, and there was no acknowledgment of responsibility from any quarter for what had happened. This presented a perfect opportunity for Labour's new leader to demonstrate his formidable skills as a parliamentary debater. 'No one resigns – at least, not yet – and no one takes the blame,' John Smith told the Commons. Under John Major, Britain had 'a not-me-guv government'.

One of John Major's election promises on taxation had been to cut taxes 'year on year', but the deepening recession forced the Chancellor to raise taxes significantly. The government had to admit that Tory tax rises would amount to the equivalent of a 7p increase in income tax, or an extra £1160 tax a year for the typical family. This figure was more than the £1000 tax per family bombshell the Tory tabloids and propagandists had predicted if Labour won the 1992 election, a fact that Labour lost no opportunity in pointing out to the electorate.

With the economic recession still taking its political toll, the government faced opposition not just from Labour but from within its own ranks. The battleground was Europe. The government won the first round of Commons votes in November 1992 on the Maastricht Treaty, with its provisions for closer European union, but by a majority of only 3 after 26 Tory MPs defied the whips. It was Liberal Democrat support that saved John Major, who had indicated that he would resign if the vote was lost. But the government was defeated in a further vote in March 1993, and this was followed in July by another setback, when 23 Tory MPs joined Labour members in the lobbies on a vote on the Social Chapter. The defeat was hugely embarrassing for Major, now widely seen as a weak and indecisive leader. Norman Lamont, in a dramatic and bitter resignation speech after being sacked as Chancellor, described a government that seemed to be 'in office but not in power'.

Already the most unpopular leader on record, worse was still to come for John Major. In October 1993, trying to reclaim the political initiative, he called for a return to traditional values and an end to fashionable theories, a move 'back to basics' in public life and private

Smith Reviews Major's Performance

In response to the plummeting popularity of the administration itself, revealed at Newbury and in the shire county elections, we have the Prime Minister's botched reshuffle. If we were to offer that tale of events to the BBC light entertainment department as a script for a programme, I think that the producers of 'Yes Minister' would have turned it down as hopelessly over the top. It might have even been too much for 'Some Mothers Do 'Ave Them'.

The tragedy for us all is that it is really happening – it is fact, not fiction. The man with the non-Midas touch is in charge. It is no wonder that we live in a country where the Grand National does not start and hotels fall into the sea.

John Smith, in the House of Commons, 9 June 1993, a few moments after Norman Lamont's resignation speech morality. This attempt to restore his authority immediately backfired as a series of damaging revelations in tabloid newspapers about the private lives of Tory MPs produced a crop of enforced resignations from his government. The whole issue of sleaze in public life moved rapidly up the political agenda, and over the next two years there was more embarrassment for the government in allegations about Westminster Council's homes-for-votes policy, arms sales to Iraq and Tory MPs taking money for asking parliamentary questions.

So transformed was the political situation and the standing of the parties that, by the time of the May 1994 local elections, Labour's memories of the post-election morning of 10 April 1992 had almost been erased. Labour was now significantly ahead of the Conservatives, who suffered their worst local elections than ever before, losing 430 seats and 18 councils. John Smith was jubilant: 'Labour has done well in the south as well in the north. Labour is now a party appealing to every part of Britain and every section of society.'

On 11 May, John Smith celebrated the party's successes in the local elections at a fund-raising evening in London for party supporters and business people. On top form, he mocked John Major's record of disasters and crises which had made him 'the Captain Mainwaring of British politics'. But his speech also carried the serious message that Labour was ready to take office: 'A chance to serve, that is all we ask.'

This event was John Smith's last public appearance. Early the next morning he suffered a severe heart attack and died shortly afterwards. As the news broke across the country, thousands of people sent messages and flowers to Labour's offices at Walworth Road, where some party workers, who had spent the previous evening with John Smith, arrived still unaware of the tragic news. The party and the nation were shocked and deeply moved.

As in 1963 with Hugh Gaitskell's death, the Labour Party had again lost a leader on the verge of power. But John Smith's death was not only the loss of a future Prime Minister, it was also the loss of a conspicuously decent man. As Labour's Lord Archer put it, Smith was the 'crusader who articulated what ordinary people understood, the protester with the gravitas of a statesman, and the political strategist whose integrity was unquestioned'. After his funeral in Edinburgh, an occasion of grief and remembrance across the nation, Labour's lost leader was buried on his beloved island of Iona.

Impending European elections postponed an immediate leadership election, but this could not prevent intense speculation over the succession, both in the media and within the party. The most likely challengers appeared to be the modernisers Gordon Brown and Tony Blair, and the traditionalists Margaret Beckett (acting as leader in the period after John Smith's death) and John Prescott. However before the leadership campaign opened, Gordon Brown announced that he would not be standing. There had been concern in some quarters that, with both Blair and Brown on the ballot form, the modernisers' vote would be split. Brown, therefore, stood aside and left the field open for his friend and ally Tony Blair.

The new Labour leader

In the wake of the outstandingly successful European election results, Labour's leadership contest began in earnest. Blair, Prescott and Beckett stood for the leadership, with Prescott and Beckett also standing for the

'Our job is to honour the past but not to live in it.' The election of Tony Blair, born in 1953, as Labour's youngest ever leader, was a clear mandate for radical modernisation of the Labour Party. Entering parliament in 1983, and Shadow Home Secretary under John Smith, he wanted to free Labour from the debris of old battles.

deputy leadership. This was the first leadership contest to be conducted under the new rules of One Member, One Vote which Smith had risked his political career to achieve. Furthermore, in respect for John Smith's memory the election for his successor was conducted in a markedly non-divisive manner.

The result was decisive, with Tony Blair winning in every section of the electoral college. Though Margaret Beckett came second, narrowly ahead of John Prescott, Prescott won the deputy leadership contest with 57 per cent to Beckett's 43 per cent.

Tony Blair's election as leader was significant for many reasons. Only forty-one, he was the youngest ever leader of the Labour Party. His youthful and dynamic style gave him an immediate appeal. He was also untainted by the party's ancestral strife that had done it so much damage. But Blair also brought to the party a strong sense of community values. As Shadow Home Secretary, his view of socialism as a strong society had reclaimed for Labour a credibility on the issue of law and order, long the preserve of the Conservatives. His phrase 'tough on crime, tough on the causes of crime' (although much satirised) came to epitomise Labour's new approach.

Most significant of all, Blair was elected as a radical moderniser. He was not constrained by political debts to different sections of the party,

John Prescott, Labour's deputy leader, was seen as a party traditionalist. After working as an official in the National Union of Seamen, he had been MP for Hull since 1970. His powerful endorsement of Smith's proposal for One Member, One Vote in the 1993 conference was crucial.

nor did he see his role as primarily one of compromise or unity, unlike some of his predecessors. Instead he believed the party needed further radical reform if it was to be elected, and felt that it was the responsibility of leadership to drive that process. Blair's leadership election statement ('Change and National Renewal') could not have been clearer about his commitment to this policy. As he put it, the message from four election defeats was that the electorate 'have told us to rethink and to review, to come back with a new prospectus for a new government. For our generation and our time, Labour must exist not only to defend the gains of the past, but to forge a new future for itself and our country. Our job is to honour the past but not to live in it.'

Yet despite this clear modernising commitment, few of those packed into the Blackpool Winter Gardens in 1994 to hear the new leader's first speech to conference could have been expecting what was to come. Blair set out the themes for a Labour government: opportunity, responsibility, fairness and trust. But there was a sting in the tail. In the last few minutes of the speech, Blair left the pre-issued script and told his party that it would only change the country if it was first prepared to change itself. This meant the revision of the most sacred of all Labour's traditional icons: Clause IV (Part IV) of the party's constitution.

Blair's proposal to revise Clause IV came as a bombshell. Its shock waves were felt throughout the party and the wider political world. To some, its boldness and courage would enable Blair to slay the final shibboleth of old Labour and prove decisive in defining a new Labour Party. But for others it was the final straw, a sword directed at the heart of the Labour Party and its traditional beliefs. An indication that change would not be easy came later in the same week when conference resolved to reaffirm the principles in Clause IV, albeit by the narrowest of majorities. For a time, ghosts of Gaitskell's failed attempt to revise Clause IV a quarter of a century earlier haunted Blair's supporters.

Labour prevents Post Office privatisation and VAT increases

While the Clause IV debate engaged the party, in parliament Labour was scoring some notable successes against the Conservative government. President of the Board of Trade Michael Heseltine was forced to announce the abandonment of plans to privatise the Post Office. Labour, the Communications Workers Union and popular pressure from

A Modern Party Prepared to Change the Country

Let us say what we mean and mean what we say. Not just what we are against. But what we are for. No more ditching. No more dumping. Stop saying what we don't mean. And start saying what we do mean, what we stand by, what we stand for. It is time we had a clear, up-to-date statement of the objects and objectives of our party. John Prescott and I, as leader and deputy leader, will propose such a statement to the NEC. This is a modern party living in a age of change. It requires a modern constitution that says what we are in terms the public cannot misunderstand and the Tories cannot misrepresent.

We are proud of our beliefs. So let's state them. And in terms that people will identify with in every workplace, every home, every family, every community in our country. And let this party's determination to change be the symbol of the trust they can place in us to change the country.

Tony Blair, 1994 party conference speech

voters in Tory rural heartlands came together to defend post office services, producing a policy climbdown that was a victory for Labour and a defeat for the Conservative right.

There soon followed an even more dramatic policy reversal. In 1993 the Chancellor of the Exchequer, Norman Lamont, had announced the introduction of VAT on domestic fuel and lighting at 17.5 per cent. This was to be in two stages with the tax starting at 8 per cent in April 1994 and only rising to the full rate in April 1995. While it may have seemed expedient for the government to stagger the increase, the effect was to give Labour two years to mobilise opposition. The party organised an enormous public campaign against the tax, which it claimed would hit pensioners particularly hard, and collected one and a half million signatures on a petition. When the government faced a crucial Commons vote in December 1994 on the introduction of the second stage of tax, concerted pressure was put on Conservative backbenchers in marginal seats to vote against it. With the House of Commons in a state of high tension, the government was defeated by 319 votes to 311. It was another humiliation for John Major's government and a great victory for Labour's campaign.

Shadow Chancellor Gordon Brown watches another signature being added to the petition against VAT charges on domestic fuel. Labour's campaign against a tax that would hit pensioners hardest ended in a Commons defeat for the government in 1994.

The rewriting of Clause IV

In January 1995 the proposed text of the a new Clause IV was published, to be decided in a ballot of all party members. Replacing the commitment to 'common ownership of the means of production, distribution and exchange', the new Clause IV proclaimed:

The Labour Party is a democratic socialist party. It believes that by the strength of our common endeavour we achieve more than we achieve alone, so as to create for each of us a community in which power, wealth and opportunity are in the hands of the many not the few, where the rights we enjoy reflect the duties we owe, and where we live together, freely, in a spirit of solidarity, tolerance and respect.

Tony Blair travelled up and down the country to special Labour Party meetings to argue the case for change, while local parties also debated the issue. After some initial doubts, it began to seem that the Labour leader's gamble was going to come off.

On Saturday 29 April 1995, the Labour Party held a special conference at the Methodist Central Hall in London to hear the result of the ballot to decide the party's purpose. The location was significant: it was in this same hall in 1918 that Labour pioneers had assembled to adopt the party's constitution. Blair's speech to the conference was a reminder of the successes already achieved under his leadership, including a membership which had risen by 100,000 in less than a year, but this was presented as only the preliminary to the success yet to come. In the Clause IV ballot, the new statement of purpose had been backed by all sections of the Labour Party, including almost every constituency which had balloted its members.

This vote was a defining moment in the history of the Labour Party. In his speech to the conference, Blair argued that, far from abandoning its past, the party had returned to its traditional

Labour's pressure against Conservative policies mounted as the government's ratings went on falling. In April 1996, the night before the Commons debate on the sale of Railtrack, this slogan was beamed on to the front of Victoria station in London.

In 1994 Tony Blair declared his conviction that the commitment to public ownership in Clause IV must be replaced if the party was to renew itself. He is pictured here with Gordon Brown, John Prescott and Robin Cook at the press conference in January 1995 which opened a three-week tour of the country to argue the case for a new statement of values.

values, territory that it should never have left. Having renewed the party, the task was now to renew the country:

Today a new Labour Party is being born. Our task now is nothing less than the rebirth of our nation. A new Britain. National renewal. Economic renewal so that wealth may be in the hands of the many and not the few. Democratic renewal: Labour in office, the people in power. And social renewal, so that the evils of poverty and squalor are banished for good. New Labour.

The renewal of the party, after its exclusion and self-exclusion from power for so long, had been a remarkable achievement. It confounded those who thought that the party had a past but not a future. It transformed the landscape of British politics and offered a way forward for socialist parties elsewhere. When, in July 1996, the party published *New Labour, New Life for Britain,* a draft of its manifesto for the 1997 general election, it could declare: 'We are back as the party of the people.' It could also await the people's verdict with more confidence than for a generation.

Chronology

1900 Formation of Labour Representation Committee with Ramsay MacDonald secretary
General election: Keir Hardie first LRC MP (for Merthyr Tydfil)

1901 Death of Queen Victoria. Edward VII succeeds to the throne
Taff Vale court ruling makes trade unions liable for strike damage

1903 Pact between Herbert Gladstone and MacDonald gives Labour clear run in 50 seats
Beginning of suffragette movement with setting up of Women's Social and Political Union

1905 Publication of MacDonald's *Socialism and Society*

1906 General election: 29 LRC MPs elected, including MacDonald
LRC renamed Labour Party with Keir Hardie elected chair
Liberal reforming legislation includes subsidy of school meals and reversal of Taff Vale decision
Formation of Women's Labour League

1908 Liberal government passes Old Age Pensions Act
Labour gains 12 more MPs when Miners Federation of Great Britain affiliates to Labour Party

1909 Osborne judgment prevents union subscriptions funding Labour Party
Lloyd George's 'People's Budget' proposing supertax on large incomes and land vetoed by House of Lords

1910 Two general elections: Labour wins 40 seats in February and 42 in December
Lloyd George returns to office with Labour support
Death of Edward VII. George V succeeds to throne

1911 Labour proposals for payment of MPs adopted
Act of Parliament restricts power of House of Lords
MacDonald elected chair of the Parliamentary Labour Party
National Insurance Act

1913 Trade Union Act overturns Osborne judgment

1914 Outbreak of Great War (First World War)
Arthur Henderson elected chair of PLP after MacDonald's pacifist views lead to his resignation

1915 Arthur Henderson joins Asquith's coalition government as President of the Board of Education
Death of Keir Hardie

1916 Asquith's coalition government collapses. Lloyd George forms administration with Conservative support. Liberal party splits
Many radical Liberals move to Labour
Henderson in 5-man war cabinet

1917 February Revolution in Russia
Henderson resigns from cabinet after being left standing outside 10 Downing Street
October Revolution in Russia

1918 November: end of Great War (First World War)
Representation of the People Act extends vote to all men over 21, and to ratepaying women over 30
Labour adopts new constitution
Labour's programme *Labour and the New Social Order*
General election: Labour wins 63 seats, and in second place behind Liberals in 79 seats
MacDonald's pacifism loses him Leicester seat

1919 Formation of League of Nations at Versailles conference
Government takes Britain off gold standard

1921 Unemployment at almost 1 million
Treaty with Sinn Fein gives Southern Ireland Dominion status as Irish Free State
30 Poplar councillors go to prison in protest at burden of unemployment relief

1922 General election: Lloyd George loses to Conservatives.
Labour wins 142 seats and becomes second largest party in Commons
MacDonald and Philip Snowden are returned to parliament. MacDonald elected chair of PLP
British Broadcasting Company set up, funded by licence fee of 10s

1923 December general election: Labour wins 191 seats

1924 **Labour forms minority government. Ramsay MacDonald is Labour's first Prime Minister**
Housing Act increases government aid for new housing
Insurance Act increases unemployment benefits
Article in *Workers' Weekly* calling for soldiers not to shoot strikers leads to collapse of Labour government
Zinoviev letter published during election campaign
General election: Labour wins 102 seats
Conservatives regain power with Liberals in third place

1925 Britain returns to gold standard leading to crisis for coal exports
Baldwin's government avoids miners' strike by setting up Royal Commission

1926 April: Miners go on strike against longer hours and less pay
May: 9-day General Strike in support of miners
November: miners capitulate

1927 Trade Disputes Act makes general strikes illegal and forces union members to contract into political levy

1928 Voting age for women reduced to 21

1929 Share prices crash on Wall Street
General election: Labour wins 288 seats to become largest party in Commons. Labour minority government with Ramsay MacDonald as Prime Minister.
Margaret Bondfield first woman cabinet minister
MacDonald first British PM to visit USA

1930 Unemployment rises to 1.5 million
Oswald Mosley resigns from cabinet

1931 Unemployment over 3 million
Economic crisis leads to resignation of MacDonald and his Labour government
MacDonald forms National government with Liberal and Conservative support. MacDonald, Snowden, etc. expelled from Labour Party
Arthur Henderson becomes Labour leader
General Election: only 52 official Labour MPs

Britain leaves gold standard
Publication of *Equality* by R.H. Tawney

1932 Independent Labour Party disaffiliates from Labour Party
George Lansbury elected Labour leader

1933 Hitler becomes German Chancellor

1935 Lansbury resigns. **Clement Attlee elected Labour leader,** defeating Arthur Greenwood and Herbert Morrison
General election: Labour wins 154 seats
Italy invades Abyssinia

1936 Jarrow March of unemployed to London
Death of King George V and abdication of King Edward VIII. George VI succeeds to throne
Germany annexes Austria
Germany remilitarises Rhineland
Spanish Civil War
Publication of J.M. Keynes's *The General Theory of Employment, Interest and Money*

1937 Publication of Labour's *Immediate Programme*, with proposals for improved health service, pensions and housing, and nationalisation of key industries
Death of MacDonald

1938 Unemployment at 2 million
Crisis over Czechoslovakia
Neville Chamberlain returns from Munich with peace agreement with Hitler
Labour conference endorses Hugh Dalton's statement opposing appeasement and supporting British rearmament

1939 Expulsion of Stafford Cripps and Aneurin Bevan over alliance with Popular Front
German invasion of Poland precipitates Second World War

1940 Labour refuses to join Chamberlain coalition. Winston Churchill replaces Chamberlain
Attlee (deputy prime minister), Greenwood, Dalton, Morrison and Ernest Bevin join coalition government
Withdrawal of British troops from Dunkirk
RAF win Battle of Britain
Germany begins blitz bombing of London

1941 Lend-Lease agreement with USA
House of Commons destroyed by German bomb
Germany invades Soviet Union
Japan joins Germany and Italy in 3-power pact
USA enters war after Japanese bombing of US
Pacific Fleet at Pearl Harbour

1942 Publication of Beveridge Report

1944 D-Day landings in France
Publication of Butler Education Act

1945 End of Second World War in Europe
**General election: Labour landslide and election
of first majority Labour government. Attlee is
Prime Minister.**
24 women MPs elected and 21 are Labour.
Atomic bombs destroy Hiroshima and Nagasaki
End of war with Japan
End of US Lend-Lease

1946 National Health Service Act, National Insurance
Act and National Assistance Act, and legislation
for nationalisation of coal
Bread rationing introduced
Labour cabinet gives secret agreement to
development of British atomic bomb

1947 Reintroduction of sterling convertibility, but
immediately suspended resulting in further
austerity measures
Nationalisation of electricity industry
Dalton resigns over budget leak
Britain withdraws from Palestine
India gains independence. Partition of Indian
subcontinent

1948 End of bread rationing
New legislation for National Health Service comes
into force

1949 Devaluation of pound to $2.80
Creation of North Atlantic Treaty Organisation
Representation of the People Act abolishes plural
voting

1950 Unemployment down to 400,000
General election: Labour forms government
with greatly reduced majority
Attlee is Prime Minister
Beginning of Korean War

1951 Festival of Britain
Chancellor Hugh Gaitskell's budget includes
charges for spectacles and dentures. Bevan, Harold
Wilson and John Freeman resign
Attlee dissolves parliament
General election: Conservative victory. Winston
Churchill is Prime Minister

1952 Publication of *New Fabian Essays*
Publication of Bevan's *In Place of Fear*
Death of George VI. Elizabeth II succeeds to the
throne
At Labour Party conference Attlee condemns
running of 'party within the party' meaning
Bevanite left faction
1.01 million members of the Labour Party –
highest ever total
First British atomic bomb tested

1953 End of Korean War

1954 End of food rationing

1955 Bevan has whip withdrawn over dissent on
disarmament
Churchill resigns as Prime Minister and is replaced
by Anthony Eden
General election: Conservatives win with
increased majority
Attlee resigns. **Hugh Gaitskell elected Labour
leader**

1956 Hungarian uprising defeated by Russian
intervention
Suez crisis. Gaitskell attacks Eden over Anglo-
French invasion of Egypt
Publication of Tony Crosland's *The Future of
Socialism*

1957 Eden resigns and is replaced by Harold Macmillan
Bevan condemns unilateralists for threatening to
send a Foreign Secretary 'naked into the
conference chamber'

1958 CND founded. First march from Aldermaston
nuclear weapons research station to London
Race riots in London's Notting Hill

1959 **General Election:** Conservatives increase majority
Reassessment of Labour's aims and values
Gaitskell proposes to revise Clause IV

1960 Gaitskell backs down on Clause IV with opposition from unions and constituency parties
Gaitskell defeated in conference vote on unilateral nuclear disarmament
Gaitskell challenged by Wilson for the leadership

1961 Gaitskell reverses vote on unilateralism
US sends more advisers and equipment to South Vietnam in war with communist North Vietnam
New satirical magazine *Private Eye*

1962 Committee of 100 employs civil disobedience tactics in protest against nuclear weapons
Commonwealth Immigrants Act controls entry through work and skills voucher scheme

1963 De Gaulle blocks Britain's application for membership of the European Community
Death of Gaitskell. **Harold Wilson elected Labour leader** defeating George Brown and James Callaghan
Resignation of Minister of Defence John Profumo over sex scandal
Conservative leader Macmillan resigns, replaced by Lord Home

1964 **General Election: Labour wins with small majority. Wilson is Prime Minister** and launches 'First Hundred Days' of reform
Balance of payments crisis
Creation of Department of Economic Affairs

1965 Rent Act reintroducing rent control
Redundancy Payments Act
Race Relations Act and formation of Race Relations Board
LEAs encouraged to extend comprehensive education
Suspension of death penalty
Wilson nominates Beatles for MBE
Edward Heath replaces Douglas-Home as Conservative leader
Southern Rhodesia issues Unilateral Declaration of Independence

1966 **General election: Labour wins with majority of 97. Wilson is Prime Minister**
Seamen strike over pay demands
Prices and wages freeze
England wins football's World Cup by defeating Germany at Wembley

1967 Britain devalues sterling leading to resignation of Chancellor James Callaghan
Wilson criticised for claiming 'the pound in your pocket' had not been devalued
De Gaulle vetoes Britain's second application for European membership
Private members' Bills passed providing for legal abortions and legalizing homosexuality for consenting males over 21

1968 Second Race Relations Act passed
Enoch Powell makes 'Rivers of Blood' speech
Commonwealth Immigrants Act affecting entry of Kenyan Asians to Britain
Grosvenor Square demonstration outside US Embassy in London in protest against American involvement in war in Vietnam
May riots and barricades in Paris
Prague's political 'spring' ended by Russian tanks

1969 Sectarian violence in Northern Ireland leads to intervention by British army
Publication of plans for union reforms, *In Place of Strife*. Proposals withdrawn after mounting opposition
Divorce made possible on basis of 'irretrievable breakdown of marriage'
Open University established
Voting age lowered from 21 to 18

1970 First national conference of Women's Liberation Movement
Act for equal pay for men and women for same work (voluntary until 1975)
General election: unexpected Conservative victory. Edward Heath becomes Prime Minister
Wilson stays on as Labour leader and Roy Jenkins is elected deputy

1971 Labour Party opposes terms of entry to Europe negotiated by Heath, but 69 MPs defy Labour whips and vote for European entry
Decimalisation of currency
Abolition of free milk in schools

1972 Unemployment at almost 1 million
Jenkins resigns over proposals for referendum on Europe
U-turns on economic policy by Heath government
'Bloody Sunday' in Derry, followed by direct rule of Northern Ireland from Westminster

1973   Arab/Israeli conflict breaks out, leading to world-wide oil crisis
Britain becomes member of EEC

1974   Miners' and power workers' dispute leads to three-day week
March general election: Labour largest party with 301 seats. Wilson is Prime Minister
Health and Safety at Work Act
October general election: Labour majority of only 5 seats. Wilson is Prime Minister

1975   Labour renegotiates terms of entry to Europe. Referendum on Europe backs entry by 2 to 1
Equal Opportunities Commission set up
First North Sea Oil pumped ashore

1976   Wilson resigns. **Callaghan is Prime Minister**
Sterling crisis leads to loan from International Monetary Fund and cuts in public spending
Commission for Racial Equality set up

1977   Silver Jubilee celebrations and street parties for Elizabeth II's 25 years on the throne
Labour loses majority through losses in by-elections
Defeat in motion of no confidence avoided by pact with Liberals

1978   'Winter of Discontent': Callaghan's government damaged by high-profile strikes

1979   Referendums on devolution in Scotland and Wales fail to obtain necessary 40 per cent majority
Government defeated in vote of confidence in Commons
General election: Conservative victory and Margaret Thatcher is Britain's first woman Prime Minister
Labour conference votes MPs to seek reselection during life of every parliament

1980   Over 2 million unemployed
Callaghan resigns. **Michael Foot elected Labour leader**

1981   Special Wembley Conference agrees to electoral college for the election of Labour leaders
Formation of Social Democratic Party, led by 4 former Labour cabinet members: Shirley Williams, Roy Jenkins, Bill Rodgers and David Owen

Labour Party membership down to 250,000
Tony Benn defeated in bid to replace Denis Healey as deputy leader
Riots in inner cities lead to Scarman inquiry
Women's Peace Camp set up outside Cruise missile base at Greenham Common

1982   Over 3 million unemployed
Argentinian forces invade the Falkland Islands. British troops regain control in three months
Big peace demonstration at Greenham Common

1983   **General Election:** Labour's worst defeat since the war
Foot resigns. **Neil Kinnock elected Labour leader** and Roy Hattersley deputy leader

1984   Miners' strike against proposed pit closures. Government sends in large police presence. Violence on picket lines
Conservative privatisation programme starts with British Telecom
Rate-capping of local councils introduced

1985   Miners' strike ends in defeat
Labour Party conference, Kinnock attacks Militant Tendency. Expulsion of many Militant members from Labour Party
Labour-dominated Greater London Council disbanded

1986   Labour's symbol, the red flag, replaced with red rose
Michael Heseltine and Leon Brittan resign over Westland affair
British Gas privatised

1987   **General election:** Labour heavily defeated, but ahead of Alliance
Labour Party launches policy review
Stock market crash on 'Black Monday'

1988   Benn and Eric Heffer unsuccessfully challenge Kinnock and Hattersley for Labour leadership
Labour introduces a National Membership Scheme
Publication of *Democratic Socialism: Aims and Values*

1989   Policy review completed with publication of *Meet the Challenge, Make the Change,* dropping Labour's commitment to unilateral disarmament

Labour wins greatest number of seats in elections for European Parliament

1990 Introduction of Community Charge leads to anti-Poll Tax demonstrations and riots
Geoffrey Howe's resignation precipitates leadership challenge in Conservative Party
Thatcher resigns and is succeeded by John Major

1991 Iraq's invasion of Kuwait starts Gulf War
Privatisation of electricity industry

1992 **General election:** Conservatives win with 21-seat majority
Kinnock resigns. **John Smith elected Labour leader**
Betty Boothroyd first woman Speaker of the House of Commons
'Black Wednesday' sees great speculation against pound and Britain leaves Exchange Rate Mechanism
Labour conference agrees to reduction of union block votes in conference

1993 Smith wins approval by narrow margin for One Member, One Vote in parliamentary selections
Government announces introduction of VAT on domestic fuel
Major under mounting pressure with defeats on Maastricht Treaty and controversy over 'Back to Basics' campaign

1994 Death of John Smith. **Tony Blair elected leader of Labour Party** with John Prescott as deputy
Labour makes substantial gains in local and European elections
Blair announces proposal to revise Clause IV at party conference
Plans for Post Office privatisation dropped
Government defeated on VAT increase on domestic fuel

1995 Special conference in Methodist Central Hall, London, agrees to changes in Clause IV of Labour's constitution
Union block votes at conference further reduced

1996 Sale of Railtrack in privatisation of railways
Publication of *New Labour, New Life for Britain*, in advance of 1997 election campaign

Picture Credits

Further Reading

There is now a vast literature on the Labour Party, but the following small selection fills out aspects of the story.

Addison, P. *The Road to 1945: British Politics and the Second World War*, London, 1975

Attlee, C. *The Labour Party in Perspective*, London, 1937

Barker, B. *Labour in London: A Study in Municipal Achievement*, London, 1946

Bealey, F. and **H. Pelling** *Labour and Politics 1900–1906*, Oxford, 1958

Bealey, F. *Social and Political Thought of the British Labour Party*, London, 1970

Benn, T. *Diaries: 1963–1990*, 5 vols, London, 1987–92

Bevan, A. *In Place of Fear*, London, 1952

Brockway F. *Inside the Left*, London 1942

Brown, G. and T. Wright (eds) *Values, Visions and Voices: An Anthology of Socialism*, Edinburgh, 1995

Bullock A. *The Life and Times of Ernest Bevin*, 3 vols, London 1960–83

Butler, D. and **G. Butler** *British Political Facts 1900–1994*, Basingstoke, 1994

Castle, B. *The Castle Diaries*, 2 vols, London, 1980 and 1984

Clarke, P. *Hope and Glory: Britain 1900–1990*, London, 1996

Cole, M. *The Story of Fabian Socialism*, London 1961

Crosland, A. *The Future of Socialism*, London, 1956

Crosland, S. *Tony Crosland*, London, 1982

Dalton, H. *Memoirs 1887–1945*, 2 vols, London, 1953, 1957

Davies, A.J. *To Build a New Jerusalem: The British Labour Party from Keir Hardie to Tony Blair* (revised edn), London, 1996

Foot, M. *Aneurin Bevan*, 2 vols, London, 1962 and 1973

Foote, G. *The Labour Party's Political Thought: A History*, London, 1985

Hattersley, R. *Choose Freedom: The Future for Democratic Socialism*, London, 1987

Healey, D. *The Time of My Life*, London, 1989

Jones, T. *Remaking the Labour Party: From Gaitskell to Blair*, London 1996

Kinnock, N. *Thorns and Roses: Speeches 1983–1992*, London, 1992

Laybourn, K. *The Rise of Labour*, London, 1988

MacCarthy F. *William Morris*, London 1994

MacKenzie, N. and **J.** (eds) *The Diary of Beatrice Webb*, 4 vols, London, 1982–85

Marquand, D. *Ramsay MacDonald*, London, 1977

The Progressive Dilemma, London, 1991

McKibbin, R. *The Evolution of the Labour Party: 1910–1924*, Oxford, 1974

Morgan, K. *Labour in Power 1945–1951*, Oxford, 1984

Labour People: Leaders and Lieutenants, Hardie to Kinnock (revised edn) Oxford, 1992

Pease, E. *The History of the Fabian Society*, 1916

Pelling, H. and A. Reid *A Short History of the Labour Party* (11th edn), Basingstoke, 1996

Pelling, H. *The Origins of the Labour Party 1880–1900* (2nd edn), Oxford, 1965

Phillips, G. *The Rise of the Labour Party 1893–1931*, London, 1992

Pimlott, B. *Labour and the Left in the 1930s*, Cambridge, 1977

Hugh Dalton, London, 1985

Harold Wilson, London, 1992

Pugh, M. *The Making of Modern British Politics 1867–1939*, Oxford, 1982

Reid, F. *Keir Hardie*, London, 1978

Rodgers, W. (ed.) *Hugh Gaitskell 1906–1963*, London, 1964

Shaw, E. *The Labour Party since 1945*, Oxford, 1996

Shaw, G.B. (ed.) *Fabian Essays in Socialism*, London, 1889

Smith, M. and **J. Spear** *The Changing Labour Party*, London, 1992

Tawney, R. *Equality*, London, 1931

Tracey, H. (ed.) *The British Labour Party: Its History, Growth, Policy and Leaders*, London, 1948

Williams, F. *Fifty Years March: The Rise of the Labour Party*, London, 1949

Williams, P. *Hugh Gaitskell*, Oxford, 1982

(ed.) *The Diary of Hugh Gaitskell*, London, 1983

Wilson, H. *The Labour Government 1964–1970: A Personal Record*, London, 1971

Wright, A. *British Socialism: Socialist Thought from the 1880s to the 1960s*, London, 1983

Other Useful Sources of Information

The Labour Party
John Smith House, 150 Walworth Road, London SE17

National Museum of Labour History:
Archive Centre at 103 Princess Street, Manchester M3 3ER
People's History Museum at The Pump House, Left Bank, Bridge Street, Manchester M3 3ER

People's Palace Museum
The Glasgow Green, Glasgow G40 1AT

Index